MW00967335

POWER SKITS

for Youth and Young Adults

25 Faith-awakening, Disciple-making
Drama Presentations

Scott Fogg

REVIEW AND HERALD® PUBLISHING ASSOCIATION
HAGERSTOWN, MD 21741-1119

To order additional copies of
Power Skits for Youth and Young Adults,
by
Scott Fogg,
call
1-800-765-6955.

Visit us at

www.reviewandherald.com

for information on other Review and Herald® products.

Copyright © 2006 by
Review and Herald® Publishing Association
All rights reserved

The author assumes full responsibility for the accuracy of all facts and quotations as cited in this book.

This book was
Edited by Randy Fishell
Cover design by Trent Truman
Interior design by Candy Harvey
Electronic makeup by Shirley M. Bolivar
Typeset: Palatino 12/15

PRINTED IN U.S.A.
10 09 08 07 06   5 4 3 2 1

R&H Cataloging Service
Fogg, Scott, 1980-   .
    Power skits for youth and young adults:
25 faith-awakening, disciple-making drama presentations.

    1. Skits.   Religious drama.   I. Title.

            808.82

ISBN 978-0-8280-1883-9

CONTENTS

* Running times are approximate.

INTRODUCTION

A Note From the Scriptwriter

I remember as a little kid listening to the sermon and not understanding a word that was being spoken. It really upset me, because I wanted to learn; I wanted to know what everyone was making such a fuss about. I remember not really understanding the whole "Christian thing" until I saw a skit the eighth-graders did at my church in Tranquility, New Jersey. I'd heard the Bible stories, and I knew basically what they meant, but when the kids performed a pantomime to Ray Boltz's "Watch the Lamb," I was forever changed. I finally got it.

And eventually I got to writing my own scripts.

What you're holding right now is a collection of those scripts. They have a tendency to make people laugh, sometimes cry, but very often also bless them with new understanding. And this must prove that God is working through this writer/director/actor (me), because there's nothing I have to offer that could do these things. God blessed me with a talent, and I'm simply returning it to Him.

I'm very fond of these scripts, and I hope you like them. And I know what it's like in your shoes: you're probably a director or actor searching for acceptable material for your youth group, summer camp, Sabbath school, camp meeting, vespers or Christian drama troupe. You have a very specific idea in your mind, and you just can't find what you're looking for.

That's why I am going to let you in on a little secret.

For the past 11 years I've treated every script I've written as a springboard, not a blueprint. If I could find a better way to say it, I would—and you should too. While I feel, ultimately, God was the impetus behind each of these scripts, they were written in *my* head, and thus they make the most sense to *me*. So find new ways to say and do things dramatically that reflect something of yourself and the unique needs of *your* audience. Tailor the scripts not only to your audience but to your actors as well.

What's great about this secret is that it's a marvelous tactic to use on fledgling and veteran actors alike. Your newcomers will appreciate being able to speak in a way that's more comfortable for them. (This, of course, leads to them just playing a "cooler version" of themselves on stage!) Your veteran actors will be encouraged to find the small nuances of the words and explore their character's motivation. They may find a more suitable way to deliver the line.

So have fun! And may the Lord bless you and your performances.

HOW TO USE THESE SKITS AND PLAYS

The skits and plays in *Power Skits* have been performed multiple times each. In other words, they're "field-tested" and ready to be shared with *your* audience.

You'll also notice that the collection assembled here is quite diverse in content and audience target ages. This provides you with a long-lasting resource for use in many different settings and venues.

At camp meetings, my team has created entire programs simply by piecing together various portions of these scripts. For Sabbath school use, we've found that several of the dramas work great as a link between song service and a topic of debate. Our team has also used them as lead-ins and wrap-ups for sermons. We've performed them for high school and academy programs, whether it was morning worship or evening vespers. We used the sketches and plays in youth outreach programs, as well as Bible-, prayer-, and leadership conferences. Also, for several summers now, these presentations have been used to enrich the spiritual experience of young people at summer camp. And recently we performed a skit between sets for two Christian bands!

Most of these skits and plays require very few props, making them easy to utilize virtually every setting. Most important, the scripts were written so that no matter where they're performed, the audience exits with a clearer picture of Jesus.

Frankly, I wrote these skits and plays because I was tired of performing campy, corny, and stereotypical Christian dramas (you know the ones I'm talking about—the ones with the druggie, the prostitute, and the abusive boyfriend). They have their place, but these scripts were written to address real "everyday" problems and point the viewer back to Christ.

I've included a lot of humor in these sketches. In my view, laughter is a great key to help open some people's hearts to the gospel.

Something I've always tried to do is model my scriptwriting after the parables of Jesus Christ. To me, this means making them "multi-layered"—three layers, to be exact. The first layer is aimed at the casual "passer-by," while the second layer is targeted at the nominal Christian. The third layer is written to touch the heart of the truly searching Christian. I think (and pray) that there's something here for everyone.

We live in a society that's wrapped up in the celluloid glitz of Hollywood and the music industry. My heartfelt conviction is that Christians need to stay in step with the changing times and reach young people and others where they're at, using a medium they're familiar with—in this case, drama.

1

STOP AND KNOW

THEME
Assurance
of Salvation

**PROPS AND
NECESSITIES**

☆ **None**

CAST

☆ **Young Person**
☆ **God**

(Kid kneels at center stage. God stands directly behind.)

Kid: Our Father which art in heaven, hallowed be Thy name. Thy kingdom come, Thy will be done on earth as . . . Can You even hear me? Are You even listening? I feel so alone, I feel like—would You listen to me?—an upstanding young Christian. I was baptized when I was 14. But You know the story. It didn't take me even two days to slip back into my former life. There was a time, right when I was getting baptized, that if someone came up to me and asked me if I was saved, I would have looked them right in the eye and said, "Yes, I am!" Everything felt right. Now, *nothing* feels right. I feel so alone. I feel so dirty. Am I saved? I don't know. I just don't feel it anymore.

(God lowers Himself onto one knee.)

God: I know. But you mustn't base your beliefs

on how you feel. You think I *felt* like letting my Son die? No, but I knew it had to be done. Don't let your feelings dictate your relationship with Me. Know the truth and be happy because of it. I had the entire Bible written just so that you could *know* who I am and what I'm willing to do for you. You're not perfect—you're a sinner. Only I can change that. And it's a gradual process. But we're working on it together. I'm here for you; I haven't left you. You came to Me, gave your heart to Me, and I've accepted you. Live your life knowing that as you confess your sins and live your life day by day, recommitting yourself to Me, that you are saved—even if you *feel* lousy. Even if you *feel* like I'm miles away. Stop *feeling* and *know*.

2

YOU'VE GOT CHOICES

THEME
Spiritual Choices

PROPS AND NECESSITIES

☆ None

CAST

☆ Modern-day "prodigal son"

(Young man stands indignantly just left of center stage.)

Young man: Choose your future. Choose Christ. Choose baptism. Choose a church. Choose a church family. Choose the right pastor for your kids. Choose camp meeting, Christian broadcasting network, evangelistic seminars, and children's activities. Choose a healthy lifestyle. Choose your theology. Choose vacation Bible school. Choose watching your friends have all the fun while you sit with your legs crossed and your head bowed and your hands folded. Choose sitting in that pew listening to an overweight pastor preach about the sin of appetite. Choose stuffing crackers and grape juice in your mouth without really taking in what it means. Choose becoming an elder and giving your last dollar to some drooling little brat who'll forget you exist the minute he turns away. Choose your future. Choose Christ.

(Pause for the audience to catch up and for young man to take in a breath.)

I chose not to choose Christ. I chose something else. I chose taking the money dad owed me and splitting town. I chose bar fights, hangovers, fast women, and easy promises. I chose waking up in strange places with strange people, wondering how I got there and how to get out. I chose neon lights, strobe lights, black lights, bar tenders, bar flies, loud friends, loud music, and loud nights. I chose weekends, not weekdays. I chose prison for felony charges and then months of community service. I chose marriageless sex, and I chose abortion. I chose chronic depression and addiction to uppers. Yeah, I chose something else. I chose not to choose Christ.

(Young man pauses as reality sinks in.)

I chose . . . my dad. Dad had always chosen to be godly. *But what side of God would he choose? Would he choose to burn Sodom and Gomorrah with judgment and wrath or would he choose the grace and mercy of the cross?*

Young man pauses again.

He chose the cross. And finally, I chose Christ.

3

CAREFREE, PRAYER-FREE

THEME
Prayer and Devotional Life

PROPS AND NECESSITIES

☆ 2 chairs
☆ 2 small tables
☆ 1 desk phone
☆ 1 cell phone
☆ 2 prayer journals
☆ textbooks

CAST

☆ Doug
☆ Mindy

At left of center stage: one table, chair, phone and stack of books is set up for Doug's use. The other items are set just right of center stage and will be used by Mindy.

(Doug enters from stage left. He seats himself on the chair, pulls out a phone card and dials a v-e-r-y long number. Then he waits.)

Doug: Hello? Mom? Hey, it's your number one son! How're things going? . . . Yeah. Good, good. Yeah, sorry about not calling. I just got the calling card yesterday. But my schedule—you would not believe the hiking they're having me do! From Brock Hall to the science complex to the fine arts building. . . . It's not like the uphill struggle you had barefoot in the snow when you were a child, but it's rough. Yeah, I'm taking 16 hours and working 20—no Mom, I'm still taking general ed courses. I know I'm a junior in college, Mom, but that leaves me with another year to decide, right? . . . Yes, Mom, there are quite a few attractive young women here, but no, I'm not dating anyone. . . . I know you're anxious for me to settle down and supply you with some grandchildren. But the college is now a university, which means all the young women are too smart for any of my ploys. . . . Yes, I received the Ramen Noodles you sent. I didn't realize you buy that stuff in bulk. Thanks. . . . Um, my prayer life? Oh yeah, it's . . . great. Every time I pop those noodles into the microwave, I say a prayer for my digestive system. . . . I'm trying. It's just really hard to squeeze time in for daily devotions with my schedule the way it is. . . . Well, no, I haven't exactly had time for my prayer journal.

(Doug picks up the prayer journal and opens it.)

Doug: Say *what?* You want me to read you some of it to you? Mom, it's kinda private, just between me and the Almighty. . . . What? You read part of it when I had it at home? Yeah, I 'm so sure it was an "accident". . . *(Doug sighs.)* Alright, fine. Hold on . . .

(Doug flips to the first page of the prayer journal and clears his throat.)

Doug: "September 11, 2001: Oh dear God, what is going on? Is this the beginning of the end? Are we at war? What's going to happen next? With all this chaos, I realize more than ever that we—that *I*—need You. That's why I bought this prayer journal. I'm going to rely solely on You, and record every moment of our journey together. I'll be at church every week. I will be the man You need me to be. I'm not afraid to fight these battles all alone, just make me strong." . . . Mom, stop crying—that was years ago. Things have changed. The Lord really helped me through all that. That's what's so great about Him. He's always there when you need Him. If I needed Him right now He'd—

(Doug pauses.)

Doug: What I mean is, well, things aren't bad right now. I'm just kind of neutral, coasting through school. It's not like I'm having a spiritual crisis or anything. Look, Mom, I've gotta go. Just stop worrying. When I really need God again, I'll get back down on my knees.

(Doug slowly hangs up the phone and exits. Mindy now enters from stage left and seats herself on her chair. Using her cell phone, she dials a number and waits.)

Mindy: Hi, Dad? Hey, it's your favorite daughter! How are things going? . . .

Yeah. Good, good. Yeah, sorry about not calling, but my schedule—you would not believe the hiking they're having me do! From one side of the campus to the other! It's like a three mile hike! . . . Yes, Dad, you've told me about the uphill struggle you had to take as a child barefoot in the snow. . . . My schedule? It's really rough. I'm taking 16 hours and working 20. . . . No, I'm still taking general education classes. . . . Well, yeah, there are some pretty cute guys here. . . . No, no one in particular. Yes, Dad, I know, but this isn't a college anymore—it's a university now, which means all the guys are too smart for any— Yes, I got the Pop-Tarts you sent me. I didn't realize you buy those in bulk. Thanks. . . . My prayer life? Oh, sure, it's, um, great. Every time I drop one of those Pop Tarts in the toaster, I thank God you're so sweet to me. . . . *(Giggles.)* Get it? . . . Sure I'm trying. It's just really hard to squeeze time in for daily devotions with my schedule the way it is. . . . No, I haven't had much time for my prayer journal.

(Mindy picks up her prayer journal and opens it.)

Mindy: R-read you some of it to you? Well, Dad, it's sorta private, just between me and God. What? You already read part of it? . . . Oh, I'm so sure it was "sort of an accident!" I know exactly what "sort" of an accident it was! . . . Oh, OK. Hold on . . .

(Mindy flips to the first page and clears her throat.)

Mindy: "November 11: Lord, You've brought me this far; will You turn Your back on me now? I came here because You led me to believe that You wanted me here at this school. And now I don't have the money to come back next semester. I trust You though. If You want me here, You will help me find the money. But Lord, You'd better hurry! Twenty-five hundred dollars. That's a whole lot of money when you don't have a penny of it. Open those storehouses and help me fill my bank account! I trust you, God." . . . Dad, stop crying. Yes, the Lord surely does bless us. He sent us that check and here I am. No doubt, God leads His people. But thank goodness things have changed—my account's all paid up. I totally agree, Dad. That's what is so cool about Him—He's always there when you need Him. If I needed Him right now, He'd—

(Mindy pauses.)

Mindy: Well, things aren't bad right now. I'm just kind of coasting through school. I mean, it's not like I'm having a financial crisis or anything. . . .

Oh, hey, I've gotta go. . . . Dad, stop worrying. When I need Him again, I'll get back down on my knees.

(Mindy thoughtfully pushes the cell phone button and exits.)

4

A SISTER'S RANT

THEME
Spiritual
Authenticity

**PROPS AND
NECESSITIES**

☆ None

CAST

☆ Girl

*The girl takes center stage and looks at the audience
for a moment. She's got more attitude than
she knows what to do with.*

Girl: Alright, I'm here to set a few things
straight. You all need to hear what I've got
to say, so listen up—I don't chew my cab-
bage twice.

See, I been sittin' here with you, listening to your sermons, amen-ing your
prayers and, to be quite frank, yawning
through everything else. See, what you've
forgotten is that these people you talk
about from the Bible were *real*, as in "real"
real. Not real in the plastic Hollywood
celebrity sort of way. These Bible people
were real in the bad hair day, morning
breath, late nights and early mornings, too
many bills to pay, not enough money sort
of way. Take my brother for example.

They don't get more real than Peter.
My brother is like an Irish kid from Philly
that you can't ever get to shut up. He

hopped on that Jesus bandwagon lickety-split but denied Him cold. Denied Him three times. That's cold.

What kills me, and killed him, is that Peter *believed* in Jesus—totally, with all his heart. He just didn't have the backbone to stand up for Him. I think we all know what that's like. It's one thing to come here and talk the Jesus talk, sing the Jesus songs, dance the Jesus dance, but when we get "out there," everything's different. "Jesus? Jesus who? I don't know no Jesus." But guess what? There's hope for jabber-jaws and slackers like me and you.

See, my baby brother, Peter, he looked at his own situation and he didn't like it. He saw himself, the all-talk, no-action kid from Galilee, and he knew that's not the kid he wanted to be. That's when he became a man. A man of God.

I'm real proud of my lil' bro. He accomplished things in his lifetime that only God could've imagined . . . what's that take? To swallow your pride like that? It takes real despair. Real anger with yourself. Real pain. Real betrayal. Real loyalty to a real God. And real love.

There, I've said my piece.

5

OUT OF FOCUS

THEME
Devotional Life

PROPS AND NECESSITIES

☆ Bible
☆ Table
☆ Script

CAST

☆ Speaker
☆ Person 1
☆ Person 2 (a guy)
☆ Person 3 (a girl)

*Speaker stands center stage, reading script and smiling.
A Bible sits on a nearby table.*

Speaker: I just love this new sketch about staying focused in our devotional lives. *(Spots Bible and begins walking toward it.)* I think I'll introduce it with a Bible verse from—

*Person 1 interrupts Speaker as he or she dashes onto the stage.
NOTE: Insert the person's name where it says "Speaker."*

Person 1: [Speaker! Speaker!] We have major problems backstage.

Speaker: Huh? What?

Person 1: In one of our sketches, "Lazarus and the Polka-Dot Turban," Chris has to wear, of course, a polka-dot turban. But we can't find it anywhere!

Speaker: You can't find it? Anywhere?

Person 1:   Chris thinks that he may have left it at home.

Speaker: *Again?* This is the second time!

Person 1:   So what do you want to do? Wanna just forget that sketch?

Speaker: *(Sighs.)* I guess so; there's nothing else we can do.

Person 1:   So, do you want to do something else in its place?

Speaker: Well, we could do "The Blind Date." That always goes over well.

Person 1:   OK. I'll tell everybody.

Person 1 exits. Speaker again faces the audience.

Speaker: Now, if our main message about staying focused in our spiritual lives is going to connect, I need to—

Person 2 interrupts Speaker as he or she enters angrily.

Person 2:   [Speaker!] Do we have to do "The Blind Date?"

Speaker: Yes! It's the only option we have! Don't get mad at me. Blame Chris for forgetting his polka-dot turban.

Person 2:   Well, OK. But since you're not doing anything important, could you help me with a couple of lines?

Speaker: Well, I guess so. What's the problem?

Person 2:   OK, we have the opening scene. We're sittin' there, and I'm supposed to say something like "So what is she like?" And Chris answers, "Oh, she's poetry in motion!" Then Melissa enters. She's supposed to trip, roll across the stage, and fall down the stairs. Then Chris says, "OK, I lied. She's not poetry in motion. She's prattle in neutral."

Speaker: So what's the problem?

Person 2:   When she's tumbling across the stage, how am I supposed to react? No matter what I do, it never feels right. Am I supposed to scream like a sissy school girl? Am I supposed to just stare in shock? Am I supposed to barely notice? What should I do?

Speaker: I like the sissy school girl approach. Do that.

Person 2: Great. Thanks a lot.

Person 2 exits just as Person 3 enters.

Person 3: [Speaker!] I've gotta talk to you!

Speaker: Really? What's up?

Person 3: I need your advice about a guy.

Speaker: Right now?

Person 3: Yes! Backstage this great-looking guy I've talked to a few times slipped me a note. He wrote a poem for me! It's so sweet! I think he really likes me.

Speaker: Do *you* like *him?*

Person 3: Oh, I don't know . . .

Speaker: So then, why do you need to talk to me?

Person 3: He is *sooo* cute!

Speaker: Yeah, so . . . ?

Person 3: Well, there are some things you just don't pass up.

Speaker: Sounds like you've already made up your mind.

Person 3: Well, yeah, but what do you think?

Speaker: Get to know him. Friends are great.

Person 3: Oh gag me with a crescent wrench! Who wants to have friends? I've been "single" for going on three weeks!

Speaker: That *is* a record for you.

Person 3:   And it's miserable!

Speaker: Just do what you know is right.

Person 3:   *(Sarcastically.)* Oh, thanks. You're a real help.

Person 3 exits. Speaker looks a bit exasperated.

Speaker: Now, what was I doing? Huh, I can't remember. Oh well. It's almost time for our presentation on how to stay focused in your devotional life. I'd better go get ready.

Speaker exits.

6

ONCE PAID, ALWAYS PAID

THEME
Discipleship

PROPS AND NECESSITIES

✫ Counter
✫ Cash register
✫ Receipt
✫ Tin of Altoids
✫ Bag of chips
✫ $5 bill

CAST

✫ Clerk
✫ Customer 1
✫ Customer 2

A salesperson stands behind the counter.
Customers 1 and 2 approach the counter.
Customer 1 has a tin of Altoids; Customer 2 has a bag of chips.

Salesperson: Good morning. Did you find everything alright?

The salesperson rings up the Altoids.

Customer 1: Yes, thank-you.

Salesperson: Your total comes to $2.19.

Customer 1 pays; salesperson provides receipt.

Salesperson: Thanks for shopping at [enter store name].

Customer 1: You're welcome.

Salesperson: Have a great day.

Customer 1 and Customer 2 start to exit. The salesperson stops Customer 2, but Customer 1 exits.

Salesperson: *(Points to bag of chips.)* Excuse me. I don't believe you paid for that item.

Customer 2:   What? Oh, I already did.

Salesperson: Do you have a receipt?

Customer 2:   Well, no. I got them yesterday.

Salesperson: What? And you're still carrying them around?

Customer 2:   No. I'm picking them up now.

Salesperson: I'm confused.

Customer 2:   What's not to understand? I came in yesterday and bought a bag of Cool Ranch Doritos. I liked them yesterday, so I'm here for some more.

Salesperson: But you can't just take them!

Customer 2:   Sure I can. Once paid, always paid.

Salesperson: Sir, that's not how it works. If you want to call yourself a customer of this establishment, you need to have actual commerce here.

Customer 2:   Well, I'm not sure I like the sound of that.

Customer 1 reenters.

Customer 1:   I love these curiously strong mints! *(To salesperson.)* Have you tried them? Here, take one. Actually, here's another $5. Give two customers you think would enjoy them a free tin—on me! And keep the change.

Salesperson: Certainly!

Customer 1 exits.

Customer 2:   Don't tell me *that's* what you want out of me.

Salesperson: It *would* take you out of your comfort zone, wouldn't it?

Customer 2:   I'll say!

Salesperson: Well, there are plenty of opportunities for commerce here. There's a clean-up in aisle 4 and—

Customer 2:   Are you saying that I need to *earn* these chips?

Salesperson: No, but the manager would love to have you show your appreciation for being able to enjoy them.

Customer 2:   Every time?

Salesperson: Sure, and even when you're not here.

Customer 2:   Well, forget it! I'll just go somewhere else. This is too much for me.

Customer 2 storms out.

Salesperson: I was afraid of that.

7

ANIMAL CRACKERS

THEME
Spiritual Maturity

PROPS AND NECESSITIES

☆ Box of animal crackers
☆ Counter
☆ Cash register

CAST

☆ Salesperson
☆ Customer

The salesperson is busily working behind the counter, arranging things and cleaning it in general. A customer steps up to the counter, holding nothing more than a box of animal crackers.

Salesperson: I'll be right with you.

Customer: Take your time.

The salesperson finishes whatever it was that needed to be done and looks up at the customer happily.

Salesperson: Now, how may I help you?

The customer places the animal crackers on the counter.

Salesperson: Ah, yes—animal crackers. You know, you've been coming here for years—for as long as I've worked here—and all you ever buy is animal crackers.

Customer: Really? Yeah, I guess you're right.

Salesperson: Why?

Customer: Why what?

Salesperson: Why buy only animal crackers?

Customer: *(Trying to be funny.)* I'm not even sure if they're crackers. I think they're more like cookies. For me the defining characteristic of what makes a cracker a cracker is being able to put cheese on it.

Salesperson: Come on, what's the real reason?

Customer: Oh, I don't know. I guess I just know what I like.

Salesperson: But haven't you ever wondered what else we have here for you?

Customer: Not really.

Salesperson: I'm just saying that the only people who buy animal crackers are kids or parents buying them for their kids.

Customer: How do you know I'm not taking these home to my baby?

Salesperson: Are you?

Customer: No, but I don't see how that's any of your business.

Salesperson: It's just a little weird, that's all. Do you like being spoon-fed?

Customer: What?

Salesperson: Maybe it's time you graduated from animal crackers to something like, oh, I don't know, corn chips? We have some pretty intense flavors.

Customer: What are you talking about, and why are you doing this to me? I just want to be able to come in here, get my animal crackers, and leave.

Salesperson: Well, I'm sorry, but the customer is priority number one in an establishment such as this. I'm just trying to look out for your well-being. The fact is, I don't think you're buying the animal crackers because of their preferred flavor, but for their familiarity.

Customer: I like what I have!

Salesperson: Yeah, but it's not what you need—anymore. You're not a child.

Customer: These are what I want to buy, now scan them! Let me pay for them and then just let me leave!

Salesperson: How about broccoli? Have you tried our broccoli?

Customer: That is none of your business!

Salesperson: Why isn't it?

Customer: Because I don't know you!

Salesperson: You could get to know me. What's the big deal? It's just a vegetable.

Customer: I don't *want* to get to know you! I don't care what you think I need, and I don't care what else you're trying to sell. I've been coming here for years. Every week, same day, I come in here, I go to aisle 4, I pick up one box of animal crackers, I pay you for them, and I go and live my life! If this is the way you're going to treat me, I'm going to take my business elsewhere!

                     The customer storms out.

Salesperson: *(Shakes head.)* Animal crackers. Not very filling if you ask me.

8

YOU'RE NOT A LLAMA

THEME
God's Will

PROPS AND NECESSITIES

☆ 2 Chairs

CAST

☆ **Pastor**
☆ **Brian**

The pastor is seated behind his desk, reading the Bible, when Brian enters.

Pastor: Hello! Come in, come in. What can I do for you?

Brian sits down in the other chair.

Brian: Pastor, I need help.

Pastor: Hmm, I see. And what's your name?

Brian: Brian, Brian Rotca.

Pastor: Rotca? That's a very unusual name. What is that, French?

Brian: No, not French. It's made up. It's "actor" spelled backward. That's what the person who wrote this skit gave me for a last name.

Pastor: What? The scriptwriter couldn't come up with a better last name for you than *that*?

Brian: You've got it.

Pastor: That's really lame. He could have at least named you something like "Johnson" or "Smith."

Brian: Yes, well, it's Rotca.

Pastor: Well, that's OK, Greg. I can still help you. I don't—

Brian interrupts Pastor.

Brian: Brian.

Pastor: What?

Brian: My name is Brian.

Pastor: Yes, I know.

Brian: You called me Greg.

Pastor: Did I?

Brian: Yes.

Pastor: I don't think I did.

Brian: You did.

Pastor: I'm terribly sorry. It's just that I don't *know* anyone named Greg. Now, how can I help you?

Brian: Well, pastor, I just . . . I just don't know how God can use me—little ol' useless me . . .

Pastor: Rest assured: God has a plan for you.

Brian: But what can I do for Him? I mean, I have no skills or talents! See, all my friends are doing all this fantastic stuff!

Pastor: Such as?

Brian: All kinds of stuff! My friend Chris grew up to be a llama! How cool is that?

Pastor: Excuse me, did you say your friend grew up to be a *llama?*

Brian: Yeah, a llama! He's down in South America now, pulling carts and giving people rides up the Andes Mountains! But me? I'm just sitting here!

Pastor: Are you saying that you want to be a llama?

Brian: Oh, if only!

Pastor: Now listen, Mike—

Brian interrupts Pastor.

Brian: Brian.

Pastor: Brian! God may have wanted your friend to be a llama. But he didn't give you llama, uh, llamish characteristics. Take for example your opposable thumbs. You can open doors. Llamas can't do that.

Brian: Big deal! Nine and a half billion people on this earth have opposable thumbs and half of them are nitwits!

Pastor: Listen. God made you what you are. He knows you by name!

Brian: *(Under breath.)* Unlike some people . . .

Pastor: He has something special in store for *you* and only you. Maybe you'll never paint a Mona Lisa. Maybe you'll never scale Mount Everest. But you have a mix of talents that no one else has!

Brian: Are you serious?

Pastor: Of course I am.

Brian: So how do I find out what God wants of me?

Pastor: Talk to Him through prayer. Read His Word. And pay attention to what brings you joy. God will reveal His will to you step by step as you stay in touch with Him.

Brian: Wow. I'll give it a try.

Pastor: Now, is there anything else I can do for you, Clarence?

Brian: My name is Brian!

Pastor: Oops! Right! Sorry, Ryan.

Brian: *Brian,* not Ryan!

Pastor: Maybe you should go before I butcher your name anymore, Thomas.

Brian: Yeah, OK. Well, thanks a lot.

> *Brian gets up and begins to walk away and turns around.*

Brian: Oh, and Mom wants to know what time you'll be home.

Pastor: About six.

Brian: OK. And thanks again, Dad!

9

DREAM INTERVIEW

THEME
Joseph and God's Leading

PROPS AND NECESSITIES

☆ 2 Chairs
☆ Table
☆ Pad of paper
☆ Pen

CAST

☆ Joe
☆ Hillary
☆ Intern

The table is set up at center stage, with a chair at each side. Hillary enters, carrying her pad of paper. She sits down in one chair and takes in a deep breath. She's very excited. Suddenly she realizes that she needs a pen. She searches her pockets and purse, but she can't find a pen. Joe enters.

Joe: Good morning.

Hillary: Oh, Mister Vice President! Good morning.

Joe sits down opposite Hillary.

Joe: Shall we get started?

Hillary: Yes, just as soon as I . . . I, um . . . This is terribly embarrsing, but do you have a pen I could borrow?

Joe pulls out a pen and hands it to Hillary. Hillary arranges herself.

Joe: Fire away.

Hillary: My name is Hillary Lambros of SkyNet News.

Joe: I know.

Hillary: Well, Mister Vice President, as we enter what looks like will be the fourth year of this incredible drought, what does the president plan on doing about it?

Joe: Nothing.

Hillary: *Nothing?*

Joe: As hard as it may be to believe, we knew this was coming. We planned for this. We've stored up enough food to feed the entire nation and the countries surrounding us for at least three more years. We'll be fine.

Hillary: How can you be so sure?

Joe: A still small voice told me.

Hillary: *(In obvious doubt.)* OK . . .

Hillary takes notes on her notepad.

Hillary: Mister Vice President, if you don't mind me saying, you're something of a mystery to the people of this country. We never saw you or heard of you, and all of a sudden you're the VP. How did that happen? Where did you and the President first meet?

Joe: It was the night he had a bad dream. He called me in to see him.

Hillary: Why would he call *you?* Where were you?

Joe: In prison.

Hillary: *Prison!* You were in *prison?*

Joe: Yes. I'd been put there by the Secretary of Defense.

Hillary: Why?

Joe: I was his family's slave and his wife said I—

Hillary: *(Interrupting.)* You were a slave?

Joe: Yes. My brothers sold me to some slave traders who were headed this direction.

Hillary: Your brothers?

Joe: That's right. They felt a little bit guilty about throwing me down into the well, so they sold me as a slave to help pay for our father's sheep that they'd stolen.

Hillary: Whoa, whoa! Let me get this straight. You were a shepherd, then your brothers sold you into slavery—

Joe: *(Interrupting.)* After they threw me in the well.

Hillary: The Secretary of Defense buys you, his wife betrays you, you were sent to prison where the President of our country called you because he'd had a bad dream?

Joe: About cows.

Hillary: *Cows?*

Joe: They were eating each other.

A long pause follows.

Hillary: *(Annoyed.)* You think you're funny, don't you? I come here, trying to learn the facts about your life, and you waste my time with this fairy tale!

Joe: As amazing as it may sound, I'm telling you exactly what happened. A person just never knows where God's going to take you when you give your life to Him. But it's always better than where you've been.

An intern enters.

Intern: Excuse me, sir. Your brothers are back.

Joe: I wonder if they brought Ben. *(To Hillary.)* You want to come meet them? I'm going to have a little thoughtful fun with them. Afterward you can ask them if any of what I just told you was true.

Hillary: I think I will. Something tells me there's a good story somewhere in this whole thing.

Hillary follows Joe and the intern offstage.

10

MAKE IT REAL

THEME
Authentic
Christianity

PROPS AND NECESSITIES

☆ **White for Jesus**
☆ **Black for Satan**

CAST

☆ **Jesus**
☆ **Satan**
☆ **Nicole**
☆ **Director**
☆ **Music:** "In My Arms Again" by Michael W. Smith or other appropriate music

Production note: *Before the production begins, introduce the sketch as having been directed by whoever plays the part of the director. This will help make the illusion more convincing.*

Nicole is at stage right, beside Satan. Nicole is curled up in a ball. Satan has his back to the audience. Jesus is at stage left, with His back to the audience as well. If "In My Arms Again" is used, fade in the music so that it hits its full volume at 2:48 (start the fade about five seconds before this point). As soon as the music hits its mark, Satan and Jesus spin around. Nicole uncurls but remains on her knees. Satan presses in on Nicole, who is a helpless prisoner. Jesus tries to reach for Nicole, but is helpless, bound by Nicole's free will. At 3:02 the music abruptly stops and the actors freeze.

Everyone remains motionless, not knowing what to do. The director, who's sitting in the front row of the audience, jumps up.

Director: Oh, no!

The director runs to the sound booth. Actors now fall out of character.

Satan: You've got to be kidding me.

Jesus: *(To Satan.)* Quiet.

Satan: This happens every time! Why do we even try to use music?

Jesus: Because it helps the audience relate to what's going on here on stage. Music is emotional, it's—

Satan: *(Interrupting.)* You think this is helping the audience?

Nicole: It's a stupid skit anyway.

Director: *(From the sound booth area.)* We've almost got it!

Nicole: Just forget it.

> *The director comes running back up and takes her seat.*

Director: Places!

> *Everyone on stage resumes their previous pose.*

Nicole: Why is it that every Christian drama has a druggie, an alcoholic, and a prostitute?

Jesus: What?

Nicole: Are those really the problems we should be concentrating on?

Director: Why are you talking?

> *Nicole stands up. Everyone falls out of character again.*

Nicole: I'm not doing this stupid skit.

> *The director storms up on stage.*

Director: Yes you are! They put me in charge. I'm the director and you are an actor. Now act!

Nicole: But this skit doesn't solve anything! It doesn't even address real issues!

Satan: It lets them know how evil Satan is and how good God is.

Nicole: You think they don't know that? They're in church [or appropriate setting]! They're obviously aware that there's a problem.

Director: Look, this is the skit I picked out. If you were the director, you could pick out something different.

Nicole: Something real.

Jesus: What's not real about it? Jesus died for you. That's what this is about.

Nicole: But it ends with the person—me—coming to the cross. But that's never the end! That's just the beginning. After that, that's when it gets hard. That's when Satan gets scared and really starts working you over. That's when the depression sets in. That's when the eating disorders begin. That's when your friends leave you. That's when your parents get divorced. That's when—

Satan: *(Interrupting.)* Whoa, whoa, whoa. There are certain things, you know, problems and stuff, that we don't talk about in church.

Nicole: We can talk about prostitutes and alcoholics.

Jesus: Keep it nice and general and let the people decipher it.

Nicole: No.

Director: Don't underestimate the audience. They're plenty smart.

Nicole: They're not an "audience!" They're people, like us, fighting to survive! And we need to address the issues they're fighting. Because Jesus is there for them, and they need to know that. And if they mess up time and time again, He'll take them back again and again. He demands perfection, but He'll take us there. He'll never allow anything to happen to us that we can't handle with His help.

Some have already gone to the cross, and they need to be picked back up. And others are about to go there, and they need to know that the road is straight, narrow, and rocky. But God will carry them the whole way if they let Him. That's what we need to be telling them!

Director: I think you just did.

Satan: So, are we done here?

Jesus: I think so.

Director: Good job.

Everyone exits.

11

MY GOD?

THEME
Personhood
of God

PROPS AND NECESSITIES

☆ Microphone
☆ Sound System
☆ Something to simulate a telephone answering machine beep

CAST

☆ Jim
☆ Jack
☆ Jill
☆ God

Jim stands stage left; Jill is at center stage; Jack is stage right. All have their backs toward the audience. God is backstage with the microphone. Jim turns around to face the audience.

Jim:	God? I'm in a lot of trouble. Remember that project on Hawaii I told you about?

God speaks through the microphone from backstage.

God:	The one you've been putting off and putting off?
Jim:	Yeah, that one. Well, it's due tomorrow, and I haven't even started on it.
God:	I say, you are in a bit of spot, aren't you?
Jim:	I was wondering if . . . maybe You could help me out a bit?
God:	Help you? How?
Jim:	Well, you burned a bush for Moses and

sent birds with bread to Elijah, so I was hoping that maybe—

God: Hoping what? That I'd sit down and knit you a hula skirt? Do you have any idea how difficult grass is to weave?

Jim: Would palm branches be easier to work with?

God: Palm branches. Maybe you'd like some coconuts while I'm at it?

Jim: Well, you used birds with Elijah and—

God: Read the story, Jim! They were carrying bread. How is a bird supposed to carry a coconut?

Jim: I don't know, maybe two could help each other.

God: I am so sure. Like two birds get together and say, "Hey, you grab one side, and I'll get the other. We'll carry it across the Pacific Ocean to some procrastinating brat in the United States." Have you seen the size of those birds' brains? They're not exactly rocket scientists. Now maybe if they were African swallows . . . but that's out of the question. Coconuts are hard to come by in Africa. They'd have to fly from there to Hawaii and then to you. Impossible.

Jim: I thought nothing was impossible with God.

Pause.

God: Who taught you your manners? Don't you know not to talk back to those older than yourself?

Jim turns back around. Jack now turns to face the audience.

Jack: God?

Silence.

Jack: God, are You there?

Silence.

Jack: God!

God: Hello, you've reached 777-0911. I'm sorry that I wasn't here to get your prayer, but just leave a short message, the time you called, along with your name, and I'll get back with you as soon as I can. Thanks. *(Beeping sound.)*

Jack: Oh . . . well . . . I just wanted to say that I'm sorry for the way that I—

Another beep interrupts Jack. He looks disappointedly at the audience.

Jack: I hate answering machines. They never give you enough time to record your message.

Jack turns his back to the audience, and Jill now faces them.

Jill: Oh mighty, heavenly Father!

God: What do you want?

Jill: Please forgive me for—

God: You did it again, didn't you? How many times do you have to do it until you get it through your thick skull? Are you really that stupid? Use the sense I gave a mule!

Jill: Lord, I—

God: Fall to your knees and pray for deliverance! The gates of Hell are swinging open, and the fire is creeping up behind you!

Jill falls to her knees.

Jill: Most gracious, kind, and . . . loving? . . . Father?

God: I am tired of your foolishness. I've bent over backwards for you more times than I care to remember. I sent my Son down to you, He died for you, and you still go about doing everything you want to do! You haven't changed. You'll never change. Just forget about it. You'll never amount to anything. Get out of my sight.

Jill turns her back to the audience. God comes from back stage and stands at center stage.

God: Ever feel like God was mistreating you? Ever feel like He was secretly laughing at your pain? Ever feel like your prayers weren't passing the ceiling? Well, we can rest assured that everything you just saw is completely fictitious. God cares for you and loves you. He's not going to mock you. He's not going to disregard you. But He's not a "genie" who will pop up and do your every bidding. There are times God will answer "no." There will be times God will answer "Just wait, you'll see." And there'll be times God will send you a burning bush. When we pray, we must have faith that God will answer it the way *He* sees fit, which may not be the way *we* want it. But it will be the right answer—every time.

12

THE "GOOD BOOK" SHOP

THEME
Accepting
Scripture

PROPS AND NECESSITIES

☆ Pile of books
☆ Table or counter

CAST

☆ Salesperson
☆ Bob
☆ Boss

Salesperson is standing behind the counter, surrounded by books. Bob walks in.

Salesperson: May I help you?

Bob: Yes, I'm looking for a book.

Salesperson: Well then, you've come to the right place. This just happens to be a bookstore. What kind of book are you looking for?

Bob: Something thought-provoking. Easy reading that will challenge and stimulate my mind but not make me feel stupid.

Salesperson: Hmm. I'm not quite sure—

Bob: Do you have *Billy Bob Brushes His Tooth?*

Salesperson: That work hasn't been critically acclaimed as one that stimulates the mind.

Bob: Then how about *I'm Not as Think as You*

Drunk I Am?

Salesperson: By . . .

Bob: An Irishman whose name eludes me.

Salesperson: I'm afraid not. Sir, are you sure you're looking for a book that's educational? It sounds more like you're looking for a little humor. Might I suggest *I Was a Rocket Scientist Prodigy* by [insert name]?

The salesperson holds up a book and does so for each suggestion that follows.
As each title is rejected by Bob, the salesperson grows increasingly annoyed.

Bob: No, I don't think so.

Salesperson: *Mashed Potatoes Can Be Your Friend?*

Bob: No way.

Salesperson: Sure they can! Have you ever gotten into a fight with your mashed potatoes? Have your mashed potatoes ever lied to you? Stolen your remote control? Made you watch home decorating shows on HGTV, when all you really want to do is go outside and play in the fallen autumn leaves while you sing "Mary Had a Little Lamb" and scarf down a super-sized order of french fries?"

Bob: Uh . . . no . . .

Salesperson: Look, if you insist on being so uncooperative, then maybe you should just go try Barnes and Noble.

Bob notices a book on the counter.

Bob: Hey, what's that one?

Salesperson: What, this book?

Clerk holds up the book.

Bob: Yeah.

Salesperson: Actually, that happens to be our all-time best seller. We've sold more copies of this than any other book ever printed!

Bob: Ooh, then I'll take it! It must be good! What is it?

Salesperson: The Bible. I don't know why I didn't think of it before. You'll find this book informative, mentally stimulating, full of hope, and it will never make you feel stupid. It'll talk to you on a personal, friendly level.

Bob: Oh . . . well . . .

Salesperson: Is there a problem?

Bob: It's just that there's some stuff in there that I don't like.

The salesperson seems annoyed once again.

Salesperson: Such as?

Bob: Revelation.

Salesperson now grows quite angry and sarcastic.

Salesperson: Right! Revelation! No beasts for you!

The salesperson tears (or cuts) pages out of the back of the book, letting the pages fly.

Bob: And I don't like Job.

Salesperson: Ah, Job! Irrelevant ancient history!

The salesperson tears out pages from the middle of the book.

Bob: I'm not wild about First Corinthians either.

Salesperson: Who needs it? We have another Corinthians! A bit overkill having two, isn't it? Let's get rid of one of those Thessalonians and maybe one or two letters from John while we're at it!

The salesperson tears out more pages.

Salesperson: Anything else?

Bob: Yeah, Numbers and Deuteronomy.

Salesperson: Say no more!

The clerk tears out more pages.

Salesperson: There you go! The Bible as you like it—now buy it!

Bob grows indignant.

Bob: I can't buy this book; it's damaged.

Salesperson: That's it! I've had just about enough of you. I'm calling my manager person. *MANAGER PERSON!*

The boss walks onto stage.

Boss: Yes?

Salesperson: This guy came in here, made all these demands, being very rude and uncooperative. Then he asks for the Bible. But he doesn't like some of the stuff that's in it, so I remove the offensive material. Now he doesn't want to buy the book because he says it's damaged!

Boss: Well, it *is* damaged. Look, you can't pick and choose what you want to believe from the Bible. Do you think God just threw things in there for the fun of it? Everything in that book is in there for a reason. So you take all of it, or none of it.

Bob and salesperson stare at each other.

**Bob and
Salesperson:**   Oh . . .

Boss: (*To Bob.*) So what have you decided?

Bob: (*Pauses.*) I don't think so; the print is way too small . . .

Boss's face reflects chagrin as he looks toward audience and shrugs shoulders; salesperson throws up hands in frustration and stomps off.

13

AND THE DEW CAME DOWN

THEME
Repentance, Noah's Flood

PROPS AND NECESSITIES

- ☆ Bible costumes
- ☆ Buckets of water
- ☆ Offstage microphone

CAST

- ☆ Narrator/God
- ☆ Noah
- ☆ Heckler 1
- ☆ Heckler 2
- ☆ Prop person

Narrator: Long ago, in a time before cell phones, rubber duckies, and megalomaniac Hollywood film directors, there lived a guy named Noah.

Noah enters and stands at center stage.

Narrator: Now "Noah" is a very unique name. Do you mind telling us how you got it?

Noah: No, not at all.

Long pause.

Narrator: So how did you get it?

Noah: My parents gave it to me.

Narrator: And how did they come up with it?

Noah: Well, they combined their two reactions when they found out my mom was pregnant. She said "Nooooooo!" while my stunned father just kept saying "Uh . . ." There you have it—Noah.

Narrator: Now Noah was a pretty good guy. In fact, he was really the only good guy there was at the time.

Noah kneels in prayer.

Noah: God, it's me again. I just want You to know that You can use me for anything You want. I'm Your man.

God: Look around you, Noah.

Noah looks around the audience.

Noah: It's not a pretty picture, Lord.

God: I can't believe it's come to this, but I actually regret having ever made humankind. They go about their lives with no concern for each other. They only care about themselves and their happiness. Not a single pure thought is among them.

Noah: What do You want me to do, Lord?

God: I'm going to clean the earth. Scrub out all this sin and start over. Otherwise, there is no hope for them.

Noah: How will You do this, Lord?

The prop dude runs across the stage and heaves a bucket of water on Noah.

God: With water.

Noah: *(To prop dude.)* Not yet!

The prop person, embarrassed, runs back off stage. Hecklers 1 and 2 enter.

God: And you need to make a boat. A big boat. Really big. Like, big enough to hold your family, two of every unclean animal and seven of every clean one.

Noah: Uh-huh.

God: I'll fax you the blueprints.

Noah: Gotcha.

Heckler 1:   *(To Noah.)* What are you doing?

Heckler 2:   *(Also to Noah.)* Talking to yourself again?

Noah: Actually, I was praying.

Heckler 1:   To who? There's nobody here.

Heckler 2:   But this is a really nice place to set up one of our gods. Why don't we bring that big bronze one over and set it up here?

Heckler 1:   Which bronze one—the elephant?

Heckler 2:   No, the one with the seven arms and the pig nose and the monkey face.

God: Tell them, Noah.

Noah: Everyone on earth has become a big problem, and God will not stand for it anymore. He's going to—

Heckler 2:   *(Interrupting.)* Which god? The god you were talking to who isn't here? A wooden god could at least give you a splinter; a bronze god could tip over on you. What's yours going to do—blow us over?

Heckler 1:   *(Sarcastically.)* Ooh, look at me! I'm the invisible god! I'm scary! Obey me!

Noah: Actually—

The prop person runs out and throws another bucket of water on Noah.

Noah: *(To prop dude.)* Not yet! *(Pause for laughter.)* He will send rain.

Heckler 2:   *(Truly disturbed, as is Heckler 1.)* No, not rain! Wait, what's rain?

Noah: Do you remember the dew that's on the plants every morning?

Heckler 2:   I do.

Heckler 1:   I do too!

Noah: Rain is a whole bunch of dew. Like, so much dew it'll cover the mountains.

Heckler 1:   That's a lot of dew.

Heckler 2:   So this . . . mountain dew . . . where's it going to come from?

Prop person comes running out with another bucket of water.

Noah: *(Forcefully.)* No!

Prop person, defeated, goes back off stage.

Noah: *(To the hecklers.)* The dew will fall from the sky.

Heckler 2:   The sky?

Noah: Yes. And it's going to shoot out of the ground.

Heckler 1:   Noah, has anyone ever told you that you're crazy?

Noah: I get that a lot.

Heckler 1:   Not surprising.

Noah: Look, I'm serious. You can either get on God's boat and live or you can stay here and get wet.

All wait and nothing happens. Noah clears his throat.

Noah: *(Louder.)* I said, You can either get on God's boat and live or you can stay here and get wet.

Still nothing happens.

Noah: *(Still louder, punctuating each phrase.)* I said, Or! You can stay here! And get wet!

Prop dude comes running out and splashes Noah with another bucket of water.

Noah: *(Upset, points to hecklers.)* On them! You're supposed to splash them! I'm

Noah! I don't get wet. I'm not supposed to get wet!

Frustrated, Noah walks offstage.

Heckler 1: *(To Heckler 2 while shaking head.)* Noah's wacky, but can you believe that prop guy/girl?

Heckler 2: *(Chuckles.)* Yeah, some people just don't get it, do they?

(Hecklers both exit, shaking their heads.)

14

GET A CLUE

THEME
Personal
Testimony

PROPS AND NECESSITIES

☆ Judge's stand
☆ Defense table
☆ Witness stand

CAST

☆ Mrs. Smith
☆ Judge Maynard
☆ Colonel Mustard
☆ Randal
☆ Algy
☆ Plumb

*Judge Maynard is seated behind his judge's
"bench" (stand). Randal and Colonel Mustard
are sitting to one side. Mrs. Smith stands at Algy's side.*

Mrs. Smith: The defense calls Colonel Mustard to the stand.

Colonel Mustard rises and takes the stand.

Judge: Do you swear to tell the truth, the whole truth, and nothing but the truth, so help you God?

Mustard: I do.

Mrs. Smith: Colonel Mustard, do you recall where you were on the night of January 18?

Mustard: I do.

Mrs. Smith: And where was that?

Mustard: Deep Creek Manor.

Mrs. Smith: And why were you there?

Mustard: Algy had invited me for cucumber sandwiches.

Mrs. Smith: And by "Algy," you mean the defendant, Professor Algernon Plumb?

Mustard: Yes.

Mrs. Smith: Why don't you recite to the court the events of that night, January 18, as best as you recall?

Mustard: It was a dark and stormy night. Algy wanted to throw a self-congratulatory party for his recent engagement to my cousin, Cecily. Most of his friends—and all of his enemies—had been invited, and all who were invited showed up. This social—but not quite civil—engagement got off to a bumpy start. I blamed Algy's choice of Bulgarian polka music for this, but by nine o'clock the party was in full swing. That's when, as fate would have it, the unthinkable happened: we ran out of bean dip. Beatrice, the family's loyal, deaf servant was charged with refilling the pewter bowl. Suddenly the lightning flashed and the thunder cracked. We were plunged into the thickest darkness I have ever seen. You couldn't see anything, not even five inches from the tip of your nose! When the lights were restored, not 20 seconds later, the late Miss Peacock was found in the observatory.

Mrs. Smith: And where was Professor Plumb—"Algy"—at this time?

Mustard: He never left my side.

Mrs. Smith: And you're sure of this?

Mustard: Absolutely positive.

Mrs. Smith: It's not at all possible that during that twenty seconds of darkness, that the two of you were separated long enough for him to commit the deed in question?

Mustard: No, for I recall that as the lights did go out, he let out a shriek. And I took hold of him, for I thought he was one of my lady friends, Miss Antwerp of Rhode Island. He shrieked again and demanded that I unloose him. It was then that I recognized the voice of my best friend. Clutching one another's tailcoats, we set about the task of finding a flashlight or a candlestick. The lights then came back on. Algy had never left my side.

Mrs. Smith: And where were the two of you located at the time?

Mustard: Right beside each other.

Mrs. Smith: In the manor.

Mustard: Yes.

Mrs. Smith: No, *where* in the manor were the two of you located?

Mustard: The Billiards Hall.

Mrs. Smith: And let us reiterate the fact that the late Miss Peacock was found in the observatory, which, while being just down the corridor from the Billiards Hall, is too far to travel in the 20-second time frame the defendant had from when the lights went out to when the lights came back on. Twenty seconds to leave the Billiards Hall, run down to the Observatory, find Miss Peacock, and commit the dastardly act and return to the good Colonel's side. All this in the most intense darkness that Corduroy County has seen in 15 years, no less. No further questions, your honor.

Judge: The witness may step down. Call your next witness.

Mrs. Smith: The defense calls Randal R. Graves to the stand.

Pause for a couple of beats.

Randal: I'm not going up there.

Long pause.

Mrs. Smith: Excuse me?

Randal: I can't get up there and do what he just did. That was amazing! He's like the star witness! He should get an award for that performance! An Oscar, an Emmy, or something. I haven't seen acting like that for years! Way to go, buddy.

Mustard: I simply told the truth.

Randal: And we applaud you!

Mrs. Smith: You need to take the stand. *Now.*

Randal: You don't need me. I wasn't even there.

Mrs. Smith: We need you to establish the trustworthiness of the defendant.

Randal: Algy? He's a great guy.

Mrs. Smith: We need you to tell that to the court.

Randal: All I'm saying is that with this guy's testimony *(Gestures toward Colonel Mustard.)*, who needs *my* testimony? He covered all the important facts. What can I add that could make any difference?

Mrs. Smith: This is not the time or place for courtroom melodrama. You know things about Algy—

Randal: *(Interrupting.)* The defendant.

Mrs. Smith: —that nobody else knows. You know a side of him that the court needs to hear.

Algy: Randal, buddy. Just because your testimony is a little less glorious than the colonel's doesn't make it any less real. Could you be a pal and take the stand?

Randal: But this guy's performance!

Algy: He did his part. That's him. I need you. I need you to do your part.

Judge: Counselor, is there a problem?

Mrs. Smith: One moment, your honor. *(Turns to Randal.)* Look, if you don't get up there and share with the court what you know, you're no good to us. You may as well be on the other side. Because if you're not helping us, you're fighting against us.

Pause for a couple of beats while Randal ponders Mrs. Smith's words.

Randal: Alright, I will.

Randal takes the stand.

Judge: Do you swear to tell the truth, the whole truth, and nothing but the truth, so help you God?

Randal: I do.

15

JESUS IS COLOR BLIND

PROPS AND NECESSITIES

✫ White outfit for Jesus
✫ Purple shirt
✫ Green shirt
✫ Red shirt
✫ Blue shirt
✫ Matching outfits for Purple, Green, Red, and Blue
✫ Jacket
✫ Microphone for narrator

CAST

✫ Narrator
✫ Jesus
✫ Purple
✫ Green
✫ Red
✫ Blue

Jesus' back is to the audience. Between Him and the audience is Purple, Green, Red, and Blue. They are lying on the floor in their matching outfits. The purple, green, red, and blue shirts are in a pile at stage right. The narrator is offstage with the microphone.

Narrator: In the beginning, God created the heavens and the earth.

Jesus turns around and with a wide sweeping motion creates the heavens. He then forms bushes, trees, and other wildlife.

Narrator: And it was good.

Jesus nods approvingly.

Narrator: In the beginning, God created man and woman.

Jesus steps between the audience and Purple, Green, Red, and Blue. He bends down low and slowly draws them up. The four stand simultaneously.

Narrator: And they were good.

Purple, Green, Red, and Blue stand in awe of all that Jesus has made.
Jesus steps back and watches them with approval.

Narrator: But one day, one of His creations got the idea that it would be funny if he tricked one of them into stealing . . .

Blue turns to Green and pulls her aside.

Blue: C'mon! No one's looking! No one will know! Just do it! One little sample won't hurt!

Green reaches up, plucks an apple, and takes a bite. Green stumbles back and falls to her knees.

Green: I—I'm cold!

Narrator: Sin entered the world, and swept across the earth like an all-consuming wildfire. No one was spared and nothing went untouched.

Blue tosses Green the green shirt. She puts it on. Blue puts on the blue shirt.
Red puts on the red shirt; Purple puts on the purple shirt.

Narrator: They were stripped of their robes of righteousness. But God had formed a plan to save each and every one of them.

Jesus bows His head in sorrow and falls to His knees.

Blue: OK, so it's not as great as the robe I used to wear, but of all the different colors I could have gotten stuck with, I think blue's the best.

Purple puts on a jacket, to hide color.

Red: Whatever. Red is by far the easiest to work with.

Green: Green is the color of choice if you have any sense of class.

Blue, Red, and Green turn to Purple.

Red: Well? What's *your* color?

Purple: My color?

Green: Does it matter? We all know that God will take these colors away from us, if we'll let Him. It's just that it's easier for Him to remove green.

Blue: Green? The color of grass stains? I don't think so.

Red: You know what I think? I think that all of these colors can be removed with no problem at all. God can remove green and blue just as easily as He can red!

Green: Ya' think so?

Red: I know so! It's not like it's purple or something!

Blue: Amen to that! Of all the colors I could have been given, I'm glad mine's not purple!

Green, Red, and Blue turn to Purple.

Green: Hey, pal. What's your color?

Purple: I don't think it really matters. I mean God will take them all away, right?

Red: Well, yeah, I guess so.

Purple: We each have these colors because of Satan, right?

Blue: Yeah, that's one way of looking at it.

Purple: We all agree that none of us asked for any of these colors. But we've got them until God changes us forever.

Green: Yeah, yeah. We all agree. So what's your color?

Purple undoes his jacket, takes it off, and reveals his purple shirt. Blue, Green, and Red all step back suddenly and abruptly.

Purple: What?

Red: You just stay away from us with that purple on!

Blue: How repulsive!

Green: How disgusting!

Red: How vile!

Jesus slowly begins to rise from His knees.

Purple: I . . . I don't understand.

Blue points to the opposite side of the stage.

Blue: Go over there!

Green: And don't even look at us!

Red: Get away!

Purple: But didn't God create us all?

Green, Red, and Blue turn their backs on Purple. Purple crumples on stage left in total despair.

Narrator: God loved the world so much that He sent His one and only Son.

*Jesus stands at center stage, reaching toward the two groups of people.
He goes to Green, Red, and Blue. They turn around. Jesus points to Purple.*

Red: Him, Lord? You want us to *love him?*

Green: But, he's purple!

Blue: I can understand blue, red, and even green! But purple? How can I love
                    someone who's purple?

*Jesus goes to Purple and lifts him up. Purple looks at Him, and Jesus holds out His hands.
Purple looks down at his shirt and takes it off. Handing it over, Purple watches as Jesus
puts on the purple shirt. Jesus then goes to Red. Holding out His hands, Jesus waits
until Red takes off the shirt and gives it to Him. Jesus puts on the red shirt.
Blue and Green take off their shirts and humbly hand their shirts to Jesus.
Jesus puts on the green shirt and then the blue shirt.*

Jesus: Do you see it now? You're all the same!

Purple smiles broadly. Green, Red, and Blue look

amongst themselves, happy to be rid of their former shirts.

Jesus: Now why don't you love one another?

Jesus holds out His arms to draw the four together.

Red: But Lord, he was purple!

Jesus: But I've taken that away.

Green: No!

Blue: He hasn't changed! Deep down, he's still purple! He'll make us all purple!

Jesus: No. Don't you understand? *(He holds up the shirts.)* All are equal in the eyes of Heaven.

Red: *(Thoughtfully.)* It can't be true!

Red, Green, and Blue turn on Jesus. Purple watches in horror. Blue, Green, and Red push Jesus around and then fix Him in the crucifixion position. Jesus is distressed as Green, Red, and Blue walk off stage. Jesus then dies, and Purple falls to his knees at Jesus' feet.

Narrator: Jesus is color blind.

16

JUST LET GOD SAVE YOU

THEME
Salvation

PROPS AND NECESSITIES

✩ Chair
✩ Rope

CAST

✩ Norman
✩ Kyle
✩ God

Norman is relaxing in his favorite chair when his best friend Kyle enters.

Kyle: Norman! There's a flood a-comin'.

Norman: What?

Kyle: A flood!

Norman: A flood?

Kyle: A flood!

Norman: Now?

Kyle: Well not yet. But soon.

Norman: I suppose we should pray about this.

Kyle: Okay.

The two friends kneel.

Norman: Dear God. My Friend here tells me a mighty flood is coming and is going to sweep away all that I hold dear, all that I love, everything that I have assembled to represent myself and my life to my visitors.

Kyle: I said that?

Norman: Lord, I don't know why the flood is coming; why You would allow this to happen. But I trust You, Lord. I know you will save me. I put my life in Your hands. You will not let me drown.

Kyle: Actually, He doesn't have to *let* you drown—you can do it fine by yourself. You never passed your swimming lessons, remember?

Norman: And Lord, if it's not too much trouble, save Kyle here too.

Kyle/Norman: *(In unison.)* Amen.

The two friends stand from praying and Norman sits back down in his chair.

Kyle: What are you doing? We gots to go! Let's go! Flee!

Norman: Dude, you've got serious issues with your faith.

Kyle: You know what happens when you drown? Your lungs fill with water, your skin turns blue, your entire body bloats, your skin is cold and clammy. That's not the look I'm going for.

Norman: We are *not* going to drown. We just prayed. We're good to go.

Kyle: So let's *go!*

Norman: No, God will protect us.

Kyle doesn't know what to say about this, so he begins pacing. Suddenly he notices something stage right.

Kyle: The water! It's here! It's at your front door and it ain't botherin' to knock!

Norman: Really?

Kyle: Yes!

Norman: The flood?

Kyle: Yes!

Norman: Huh. Well, maybe we should climb up onto the roof. Because, like, we'll be closer to God, and it'll be easier for him to come down and save us.

Kyle: OK—let's go!

Norman and Kyle climb up on the roof.

Kyle: So now what?

Norman: We wait.

Kyle: We wait?

Norman: We wait.

Kyle: For what?

Norman: God. He will be here anytime now.

Kyle points off stage left excitedly.

Kyle: Look! Look! It's a helicopter! We're saved! Over here! Over Here!

Kyle waves excitedly. The two "follow" the helicopter until it is right above them.

Norman: (*Talking to helicopter.*) Thank-you, but we're okay! We don't need your help! God is going to save us!

Kyle: *What?*

Norman: Dude, I am telling you, you have some serious problems with you faith.

Kyle: But the helicopter is here to save us!

Norman: No, it is a temptation from Satan. You can't trust the people in that helicopter. They do, after all, work for the government.

Kyle: *What?*

Norman:	You'll thank me later. *(To helicopter.)* Get thee away from us, helicopter! Go save the Johnsons—they're atheists!

Norman and Kyle watch the helicopter fly away. They look down.
The water level is rising, and they move to center stage, back to back.

Kyle:	We're about to be up a very deep creek.

Norman:	Nah. God will save us.

Kyle excitedly points toward stage right.

Kyle:	Look! Look! It's Bob! He's in his speedboat, and he's coming this way!

A rope is thrown from off stage right, and Kyle grabs it.

Kyle:	C'mon—we're outta here! We're saved!

Norman:	Uh, no.

Kyle:	Excuse me?

Norman:	Who's driving that boat?

Kyle:	Bob!

Norman:	Is Bob God?

Kyle:	No.

Norman:	There you have it.

Kyle:	*(Looks at Norman, then toward Bob.)* Hit it!

The rope goes taught, and Kyle is pulled offstage. Slowly Norman
backs away, quickly running out of room as the water rises.

Norman:	God, I could really use that rescue now.

God speaks from offstage.

God:	Norman, Norman. Before you even prayed, I sent you a warning. You

could have been saved then. Then you prayed for a rescue, so I sent you a helicopter. You could have been saved then. And then I sent you Bob. Oh, Norman, why didn't you let Me save you?

Norman is whisked off his feet and rolls offstage as the water carries him away.

17

DEMONS LOSE

THEME
Spiritual Warfare

PROPS AND NECESSITIES

☆ T-shirt, Yankees cap, trench Coat, (for Azrael)
☆ Business suit (for Herc)
☆ White outfit (for Gabriel)

CAST

☆ Azrael
☆ Herc
☆ Gabriel

The stage is clear. Azrael enters stage left, wearing jeans, a T-shirt, a backward Yankees cap, and a trench coat. He waits impatiently for a moment and begins pacing. Herc enters stage right, wearing a business suit. Azrael stops pacing and tries to ignore Herc. Finally Herc speaks.

Herc:	So, what are you doing here?
Azrael:	Meeting somebody. And you?
Herc:	Same.

A moment of silence passes.

Azrael:	What's it been, 10 years?
Herc:	Eight and a half.
Azrael:	Time flies when you're having fun.

(Another pause.)

Herc:	It's been a long eight years, hasn't it?

Azrael: Yeah. How ya' been?

Herc: Busy.

Azrael: You still like your work?

Herc: Not like I used to. It's harder and harder to find people you can trust. Everyone is vying for the boss's attention. They'll stab ya' in the back just to get a scrap thrown their way. Every once in a while you form an alliance, but you make sure it lasts only as long as absolutely necessary. What about you? What have you done with your life?

Azrael: *(Shrugs.)* Stuff.

Herc: See, that was always your problem. You were never a visionary.

Azrael: This coming from the one who couldn't grasp the necessity of indoor plumbing.

Herc: Hey, that was a long time ago!

> *Azrael shrugs with a "whatever" look on his face.*
> *A silent moment passes and Azrael starts laughing.*

Herc: What?

Azrael: What was the name of that girl you were with?

Herc: The last time I saw you?

Azrael: Yeah.

Herc: That would have been . . . Sarah.

Azrael: Ah, yes—Sarah. *(Laughs again.)* I was just remembering the look on her face when she found out she was pregnant.

> *(Herc joins in the laughter.)*

Herc: *(Imitating Sarah.)* "But I can't be pregnant! I'm only a freshman!"

> *They laugh as they remember. Azrael shakes his finger at Herc.*

Azrael: I gotta give you credit. I would have left it at that, let her fend for herself. But you go in for the sucker punch and see to it that the baby comes out addicted to heroin. Sheer brilliance.

Herc: I have my moments.

Azrael: I guess that's why you've made it almost to the top while I'm still down here peddling crack on the street corner.

Herc: Hey, every part is needed for the play to work.

Azrael: *(Pauses.)* Think we could ever team up?

Herc: I might be able to throw one of my clients your way.

Azrael: Hey, while you're here, do you think I could ask you a quick question?

Herc: And what's that?

Azrael: Do you ever regret it?

Herc: Regret what?

Azrael: The war.

A silent moment passes.

Herc: No. This is all His idea of justice, this is His idea of perfection. This is what He wanted! I'm not interested in serving a God who creates a massive chess game and only allows all those to play to be mere pawns. Not when you can raise yourself up through ways and means to make yourself a knight, or even a king! Was it not Milton who said "'Tis better to be a ruler in Hell than a slave in Heaven?"

Azrael: No, that was Satan.

Herc stares at Azrael for a moment.

Herc: While I might not particularly enjoy my job, it has to be done. For the good of humankind.

Azrael: I can't remember what His face looks like. It used to really bother me because I'd remember the peace, the tranquility, that I had when I knew He was there. And then it was taken from me, and the separation from Him killed me over and over again, every day, every night. But then one morning, I was walking down the Jersey shore, and it dawned on me: If this Guy is going to hold me accountable for my actions, my choices—where's the love in that? And that hollow in my heart that I thought I needed to fill with Him I filled with hatred—for Him, for all of His creatures and creations . . . everything. We have to win, you hear me? We hafta prove Him wrong!

(Gabriel enters, and the three circle each other.)

Gabriel: And proving Him wrong, I would like to point out, is something that you have failed to do for the past 6,000 years. What makes you think you'll be able to do it today or even tomorrow? What possible quarrel do you have with our Maker? You, both of you, have stood in His presence. You have seen His smile, heard His laughter, and you have seen His loneliness. What bothers you the most about Him? That He gave you a choice? That He let you go away? That He pursued you to the very gates of the city, begging you to not leave? Did it ever cross your minds that if you went back to Him right now, He'd accept you with open arms? *(Pauses.)* But that's too beneath you, isn't it?

Herc: Gabriel, don't waste your breath. We—

Azrael: Why do you do it? Why? Why do you fight day in and day out to protect and save a race of beings who have no respect for you or their Maker?

Herc: He gives them Eden . . .

Azrael: They throw it away.

Herc: He gives them His Son . . .

Azrael: They kill Him.

Herc: He sends messages, signs, and warnings . . .

Azrael: They ignore them.

(Gabriel smiles, then laughs.)

Herc: What?

Azrael: What's so funny?

Gabriel: While the two of you stood here trying to woo me over to the dark side, a couple of my boys intercepted Sean and Natalie.

Azrael: What? But I was supposed to be meeting Sean here! We had a deal!

Herc: And Natalie . . .

Gabriel: I'd say "sorry," but I'm not. And I'm not about to start lying.

Herc: One day, I swear, we will have our revenge!

Gabriel: Stop lying to yourself. You're almost as blind as godless humans. If only we could open their eyes so they could see how you demons delight in their pain. If only we could show them . . . they'd want nothing to do with you or your insidious ploys.

Azrael: *(Mockingly.)* Oh pity us . . .

Gabriel: *(Sadly, thoughtfully.)* Indeed.

(Gabriel eyes the audience as he exits stage right.)

Herc exits first, stage left. Azrael remains a moment longer, looking over the audience, and then follows Herc offstage.

18

DANNY AND THE LLAMA'S DEN

THEME
Loyalty
to God

**PROPS AND
NECESSITIES**

☆ Umbrella
☆ Alarm clock
☆ Cape

CAST

☆ Danny
☆ Donnie
☆ Debbie
☆ King Darius
☆ Llama-Man
☆ Narrator

King Darius enters with an umbrella in hand. He stands very happily. The offstage narrator begins. (The actors do not react to the narrator until the final "fateful" scene.)

Narrator: In the fifth year of the reign of King Darius . . .

(Darius opens his umbrella with a smile.)

Narrator: No, not "rain" as in precipitation! Reign, like you're the king, the Head Honcho, the Big Cheese, the Man with the Plan.

(Darius tosses the umbrella aside.)

Darius: Oh, I rule!

(Darius raises his fist in the air triumphantly.)

Narrator: Precisely. Now, as I was saying, In the fifth year of the reign of King Darius, he realized that in order to catch his favorite daytime drama, *The Young and the Rest of 'Em,* he had to finish all his kingly chores first. But how could he? He was only one man. Ah, the satraps!

Darius: Of course! Sand traps! I'll snatch a few unsuspecting peasants as they play golf, deprive them of their free will, and subject them to—

Narrator: *(Interrupting.)* No, not sand traps—satraps! The 120 governors you specifically chose to rule your provinces!

Darius: I really did that?

Narrator: And they answer to your three most trusted advisors: Donnie, Danny, and Debbie.

(Donnie, Danny, and Debbie enter and stand around Darius.)

Darius: Excellent! I'm so smart! Well . . . anybody up for another pulse-pounding, nail-biting, scandalous, adventurous episode of the *Young and the Rest of 'Em?*

Donnie: Sure!

Debbie: I love that show! Can you believe Sean left Valerie even after she woke up from the coma her evil Siamese twin—who had just returned from Mars—put her in?

Darius: Unreal!

(Darren, Donnie, and Debbie sit down around a "television.")

Danny: Uh, shouldn't we be working?

Darius: Shhh! I can't hear what Alec is saying to Trey about his intern!

Danny: But, Sire, what about the taxes?

Darius: Oh, Danny Boy! You worry too much!

Donnie: Did we bring popcorn?

Debbie: *(To Darius.)* Do you have any soft drinks available?

Danny: But, Sire, unless we raise taxes or completely stop spending money, we'll be bankrupt in roughly 14 hours.

Narrator: This alarmed the king.

(Alarm clock rings offstage.)

Darius: I am quite alarmed.

Narrator: He had no idea what to do.

Darius: I have no idea what to do.

Danny: You could raise taxes . . .

Darius: Good thinking! Are you from Washington, D.C.? From now on, I'm making you second in command . . . after the show.

*(Danny joins the others watching "TV." Donnie and
Debbie stand up and walk toward stage left.)*

Narrator: This development did not make the other advisors happy. They immediately began plotting ways to get rid of Danny.

Debbie: This does not make me happy.

Donnie: Me neither. Let's begin plotting ways to get rid of him.

Debbie: The narrator?

Donnie: No, Danny. Hey, how about we sell him to a band of bad guys going to Egypt as a slave? He could work for somebody named, oh, I don't know, Potiphar?

Debbie: What a dumb idea. That could never happen.

Donnie: Well, it's the best idea I have. I'm not hearing any good ideas coming from you!

Debbie: Wait—did you say "good idea?" I think—yeah, I just had one!

(Debbie whispers in Donnie's ear.)

Narrator: It was a perfect plan, one that could not fail. All they had to do was—

Donnie: *(Interrupting.)* Hey, quiet! Don't give it away!

Debbie: Do you think it'll work?

Donnie: Watch and learn.

(Donnie approaches Darius.)

Donnie: Seeing that it is a commercial break, O King, may we call something to your attention?

Darius: What is it, Donnie Boy?

Donnie: My lord, there are some people in your grand kingdom who would rather bow to others than to you.

Darius: That's terrible! Go do something about it. And put my seal on it, whatever it takes!

Donnie: *(Bowing.)* Yes, Darius Boy, I mean, my lord.

(Everyone leaves the stage except for Danny, who gets on his knees and begins to pray.)

Danny: Lord, please help me be the man You need me to be. Help me set an example to these people who don't know You. Help me show them Your love, Your compassion, and Your determination.

(Donnie and Debbie burst onto the scene.)

Donnie: Ah-ha!

Danny: What?

Debbie: What are you doing?

Danny: Praying.

Donnie: To whom? King Darius?

Danny: No, to God.

Debbie: Ah-ha! But surely you, the "second-in-command," heard the edict yesterday.

Donnie: Article 13-14; sub-article 6-3; column 4, paragraph 2.

Debbie: "No one shall bend their knee or pray to anyone but the king!"

Danny: I will worship only my God. I'll serve the king till the day I die, but I will only *worship* my God—no matter what you do to me.

Donnie: Anyone who breaks the law must be thrown into the Llama's Den!

(Danny grows wide-eyed. Then he suddenly grows confused.)

Danny: Wait—the *what?*

Debbie: The Llama's Den.

Danny: What happened to the lions?

Donnie: Rabies. Had to put 'em down.

Danny: Llamas? That's the best you could do?

Debbie: Not just any llamas! Ill-tempered llamas!

Donnie: Very grumpy. They spit.

Debbie: *Genetically altered,* ill-tempered llamas!

Danny: Genetically altered?

Debbie: One dude got bit and now he fights crime with all the power of the llama as Llama-Man.

(Llama-Man runs across the stage, stopping to pose briefly, and with a whisk of the cape runs offstage again, the whole time chanting, "Llama, llama, llama, llama!")

Danny: You've got to be kidding.

Debbie: We don't need all this drama!

Donnie: We're throwin' you to the llama!

(Donnie and Debbie escort Danny offstage.)

Narrator: And so it was that Danny was thrown to the llamas. But the Lord protected him. God stood up for Danny because Danny had stood up for Him. You can read what *really* happened in the Bible book of Daniel, chapter six. But this is our story, and we're sticking with it, just the way you should stick with God.

19

WHAT'S THE POINT?

THEME
Sharing
Jesus Christ

PROPS AND NECESSITIES

☆ Table
☆ 2 Chairs
☆ Director's chair
☆ Megaphone
☆ Script

CAST

☆ Actor 1
☆ Actor 2
☆ Director

The two chairs are beside the table.
The director sits in a director's chair nearby.

Director:	And . . . action!
Actor 1:	I'm bored.
Actor 2:	You said it.
Actor 1:	I mean *really* bored. You want to do something?
Actor 2:	I don't know. What do you want to do?
Actor 1:	I don't know. What do *you* want to do?
Actor 2:	I don't know. What do *you* want to do?
Director:	Cut!

The director leaps from his chair, script in hand.
Are you trying to put us to sleep?
This is the worst skit I've ever seen!

Actor 1:	Hey, you wrote it!
Director:	Did not!
Actor 1:	Did too!
Director:	Did not!
Actor 1:	Did too!
Director:	Did not!

Actor 2 snatches the script from the director's hand.

Actor 2:	This is the script you gave us. *(Points to script.)* Look right here: "Written by . . ." Whose name is that?
Director:	Mine.
Actor 2:	Okay then! If this skit is so bad, it's your fault!
Director:	Okay, fine. But this skit could be really funny.
Actor 1:	How?
Director:	Well, you could dress up like a girl.
Actor 1:	No way!
Director:	Well, then, maybe we could do something about . . . burping. That's always funny!
Actor 2:	Yeah, but we can't burp on command.

This annoys the director.

Director:	Why not? Okay, fine! One problem is that the audience can't see you very well.
Actor 2:	Really?
Director:	Yes, really. Here, try it again, standing like this

The director places them in odd-shaped stances.

Director: Great! Now . . . action!

Actor 1:   I'm bored.

Actor 2:   You said it.

Actor 1:   I mean *really* bored. You want to do something?

Actor 2:   I don't know. What do *you* want to do?

The director leaps from chair again.

Director: Cut! We can't hear you! You must speak up! Think you can do that for me? Loud? We're going to try it again, and this time, *loud!*

The director walks off stage. Actor 1 and 2 get ready for their parts again.

Director: And . . . action!

Actor 1:   *(Screaming.)* I'm bored!

Actor 2:   *(Screaming.)* You said it!

Director: Cut!

Actors cannot hear the director so continue.

Actor 1:   *(Still screaming.)* I mean *really* bored! You want to do something?

Director: *(Loudly.)* Cut!

Actor 2:   *(Screaming.)* I don't know! What do *you* want to do?

The director takes up a megaphone.

Director: Cut!

Startled, the actors scream.

Actor 1:   You don't have to yell!

Actor 2:   Yeah, man, we're right here.

Director: Alright, I think I know the problem. Annunciation. We can't understand a word of what you are saying.

Actor 1:   Annunciation? I can't even pronounce it. How am I supposed to do it?

Director: Let's go straight to the kitchen scene. Annunciate each word.

The actors go to the table and sit down. The director proceeds to make them stand in odd poses again. Finally satisfied, the director begins returning to his chair.

Director: Remember: ah-nun-ci-ate! Pronounce the words with pride! And . . . *action!*

Actor 1:   **P**lease **p**ass the **p**eppered **p**ickles, **P**aul.

(With each "p," Actor 1 showers Actor 2 with spit. Actor 2 falls back, wiping the spit from his face.)

Actor 2:   Cut!

The director storms up.

Director: What was wrong with that? It was perfect!

Actor 2:   That was my second shower today! I didn't need a second shower today!

Director: What are you talking about?

Actor 2:   He spit all over me!

Director: Well, that's a price I'm willing to pay.

Actor 1:   *(To director.)* But what's the point?

Actor 2:   Yeah, what's the message here? What are we trying to say?

Director: There is no message. It's just funny.

Actor 2:   But aren't we Christians?

Director: Yes. What about it?

Actor 2:   Isn't it our job to tell people about Jesus' love?

Director: I suppose it is.

Actor 1:   It's okay to laugh. It's okay to have fun. But we need to tell people about Jesus!

Director: Really?

Actor 2:   Really! I mean, why go through all the motions and not have anything important to say?

Actor 1:   We need a script rewrite.

Director: You know what? You're right. I'll see what I can do.

Actor 1:   Oh, and **p**lease have a **p**owerful **p**oint to the **p**lay.

The director wipes his face dry as the actors exit.

Director: Too much annunciation.

20

SLIPPERY WHEN WET MEETS DANGEROUS CURVES

THEME
Jesus'
Sacrificial
Love

PROPS AND NECESSITIES

☆ Native American costumes
☆ 2 Teepees
☆ Log
☆ Tea cups

CAST

☆ **Tiger of the Woods**
☆ **Moonwalk**
☆ **Weeping Willow**
☆ **Chief**
☆ **Slippery When Wet**
☆ **Dangerous Curves**
☆ **Gummy Worm**

Tiger of the Woods and Moonwalk are sitting on a log amid teepees. Tiger is lacing up Moonwalk's moccasin.

Tiger: Then the rabbit went around the tree not once, not twice, but three times before leaping into its hole.

Moonwalk: You are truly amazing, Tiger of the Woods.

Tiger: I do what I can, Moonwalk. But someday, you must learn to tie your own moccasins.

Moonwalk: Why can't I just get some Velcro moccasins? They're so much easier, and the ones the paleface trader has go well with my braids.

Tiger: You think we can afford Velcro? Pelts don't grow on trees!

Moonwalk: Squirrel pelts do.

Tiger: Yes, but—

Moonwalk: Beaver pelts grow *under* trees . . .

Tiger: Remember the time we dipped you in tar and stuck you to the backside of an angry water buffalo?

Moonwalk: Late at night I can still hear the mooing . . .

Tiger: It happened once. It will happen again. The only question is when.

A brave bursts onto the scene. It is Slippery When Wet, and he is badly injured.

Slippery: Help! Help me . . . please!

*Slippery When Wet collapses at their feet. Tiger of the Woods
and Moonwalk stare at him for a moment. Moonwalk turns back to Tiger.*

Moonwalk: Monkey pelts grow on trees.

Tiger: You've been drinking the fire water again, haven't you? When was the last time you saw a monkey in North America? And I'm not talking about the Shawnee Zoo.

Weeping Willow comes from the Indian Camp.

Willow: How.

Tiger: What?

Moonwalk: When?

Tiger: Where?

Willow: How.

Moonwalk: *(Pauses.)* Oh, gotcha. But that is not the newly-approved international Indian greeting.

Willow: I am *not* going to say that!

Moonwalk: You must, Weeping Willow, or we will not recognize you.

Willow: Oh come on—you can't be serious. The Cherokee used it for a while and they said it served only as a great annoyance.

Tiger: *(Pretends Weeping Willow is not present.)* Who said that?

Moonwalk: I didn't hear anything, did you?

Tiger: Just the rustling of the autumn wind, my brother.

Willow: *(Annoyed.)* Oh, fine then. *Whhaaaaasssssssuuuuup? [Or current fad greeting.]*

Tiger: *Whhaaaaasssssssuuuuup?*

Moonwalk: *Whhaaaaasssssssuuuuup?*

Willow: *(To herself.)* It's just a fad, just a fad. This too shall pass.

Tiger: Silence, squaw. Such insolence will not be tolerated.

          Weeping Willow notices the unconscious Slippery When Wet.

Willow: Who is that?

Tiger: We don't know.

Moonwalk: Nor do we care.

Willow: We can't just leave him here! We must take him back to camp! You take his arms, Moonwalk, and you take his legs, Tiger of the Woods. I will take his pulse.

          Weeping Willow takes pulse of Slippery When Wet as Tiger of the Woods
          and Moonwalk carry him back to camp. They take him into one of the teepees.
          Moments later the chief walks out of his teepee, followed by Dangerous Curves.

Chief: Dangerous Curves, how is he who was found by our scouts?

Curves: Weeping Willow has not left his side. She has spoken to no one, so there is no word on the—

Chief: *(Interrupting.)* Do not whine like mule who has lost his way in the woods on the night of a new moon. Go see Weeping Willow and tell her chief want know how brave is healing.

Curves: Yes, my chief.

Chief: But first, is there not some grass and even some dirt on my feet?

Dangerous Curves falls to her knees and begins cleaning off the chief's feet.

Curves: Has the chief ever considered purchasing some sandals or even having some moccasins crafted for him by Screeching Owl?

Chief: Silence, and know your place, squaw. Of course I have considered this. But I have high arches. No moccasin will help that, and sandals, well, my paleface squaw, simply do not go with this Seminole ensemble. Now go! Speak to Weeping Willow for me!

Dangerous Curves stands and goes to Weeping Willow's teepee.
She rings the "doorbell." Weeping Willow answers the tent flap.

Willow: Yes?

Curves: Our chief wishes to see you.

Willow: I'm busy right now.

Curves: He wants to know how the wounded man is healing.

Slippery When Wet steps out of the teepee.

Slippery: Then take me to your chief and let me speak for myself.

Willow: But we're in the middle of an herbal tea party.

(Chief approaches.)

Chief: *(To Slippery When Wet.)* Ah, brave brave! From what tribe do you hail?

Slippery: A humble Apache tribe.

Gummy Worm steps out of the chief's teepee.

Gummy: Apache? Gummy Worm no likey Apache!

Slippery: *Whhaaaaassssssuuuuup?*

Chief: *Whhaaaaasssssssuuuuup?*

Willow: *Whhaaaaasssssssuuuuup?*

Curves: *Whhaaaaasssssssuuuuup?*

Tiger of the Woods and Moonwalk step out of Weeping Willow's teepee. When they see everyone else standing around, they throw their tea cups back into the teepee and try to cover up the fact that they were just partaking in a tea party.

Tiger: *Whhaaaaasssssssuuuuup?*

Moonwalk: *Whhaaaaasssssssuuuuup?*

Gummy: Whatever.

Chief: Gummy Worm, you disgrace me. Forgive my son; he is young, dumb, and ugly. I am Chief Screams Like a Sissy School Girl With a Skinned Knee. Welcome to our tribe.

Slippery: Thank-you. I am Slippery When Wet.

Chief: Aren't we all?

Slippery: What?

Chief: Aren't we all slippery when wet?

Slippery: That is my name, Slippery When Wet.

Chief: Oh, well the yolk is on my face, like the snake that bit into the robin's egg, expecting to find a bird but instead finding it to be underdeveloped.

All appear confused regarding the chief's remarks. Dangerous Curves spots mud on the feet of Slippery When Wet. She quickly falls to her knees and begins scrubbing his feet.

Slippery: What are you doing?

Curves: I'm washing your feet.

Slippery: Why?

Curves: They are dirty.

Chief: Slippery When Wet, this is my paleface squaw servant, Dangerous Curves. I acquired her in a game of Chance.

Slippery: Poker?

Chief: No. I do not need to poke her; she serves willingly. She will wash your feet.

Slippery: But that is not a proper job for a squaw, paleface or not. Chief—

Chief: *(Interrupting.)* Please, I do not believe in titles.

Slippery: OK, Screams Like a Sissy School Girl With a Skinned Knee, I thank you for your hospitality, but I cannot have her wash my feet. I'll just wipe them off.

> *He wipes them in the grass. Everyone stares at him.*

Chief: Slippery When Wet, why do you mock me? Why will you not have my servant squaw wash your feet?

Slippery: Where I come from we treat our squaws with respect. We ask them to do nothing that we ourselves would not also do.

Chief: That's the dumbest thing I've ever heard. *(To others.)* You must not listen to this man. I can now see that his name should have been Dumb as a Bag of Rocks. Squaws, leave this man and do not speak to him. I will not have him filling your minds with gibberish.

> *The squaws leave, going into Weeping Willow's tent.*

Slippery: Please listen, Screams Like a Sissy School Girl With a Skinned Knee—

Chief: *(Interrupting.)* I am chief of this tribe.

Slippery: Chief, I mean you no harm.

Chief: Then leave us. Come men, we shall go watch the Braves game.

> *All the men exit into the chief's tent. Slippery When Wet
> is left by himself. He turns his eyes heavenward.*

Slippery: Heavenly Father, what am I to do now? I have watched this tribe from afar for a long time now, and I have seen how they treat the paleface girl. I know it is not how You would have it, and that is why I came here when You said to. But now what? What do I do now? Father, I must admit, though I've only seen her from afar until today, I think I have feelings for her.

Dangerous Curves steps out of Weeping Willow's tent.

Curves: Slippery When Wet?

Slippery: Dangerous Curves.

Curves: Did you mean . . . I mean, I don't understand. Why won't you let me wash your feet?

Slippery: You spend your life in the mud, but you were made to soar. To be lifted up on the wings of the eagle, that is where you should be. Not washing people's feet!

Curves: I am supposed to be gathering berries for tonight's feast. Would you like to come with me?

Slippery: Yes!

The two walk away together. Time passes. Moonwalk and Gummy Worm step out of the chief's tent.

Moonwalk: What is going on?

Gummy: What?

Moonwalk: Look at my feet!

Gummy: Did you walk in a pasture?

Moonwalk: Three days ago. And ever since that Apache has been here, Dangerous Curves has not been doing her job. One week he's been here now! If he's healthy enough to go on all those walks with Dangerous Curves, he's healthy enough to leave us alone!

Chief steps out of his tent.

Chief: Squaws? Oh, sorry. I thought I heard whining out here.

Moonwalk: Chief. Something must be done with Dangerous Curves. She spends so much time with Slippery When Wet that she fails to do her job. Look at these feet!

Chief: I don't have to—I can smell them.

Dangerous Curves enters.

Chief: Dangerous Curves, I must express our displeasure. Our feet reek of the fields, of bison, and of horse. Washing our feet is your job. You must not fail to do this. You think you're special because this Apache brave likes you? You're still nothing more than a paleface squaw. I own you. You will do as I tell you. You will not see Slippery When Wet ever again!

Slippery When Wet enters.

Slippery: Chief!

Chief: And you! You must leave my tribe immediately.

Slippery: Not without her.

Chief: She is not yours to take.

Slippery: I will not leave until she is free.

Curves: But you must leave me. Go!

Slippery: No.

Curves: What is your problem?

Slippery: *(Pauses.)* I love you.

Gummy: *(Sappy tone.)* Ooooooooooh!

Curves: You *love* me?

Chief: You love her? She's just a paleface squaw. Nothing special. Just a servant who doesn't know her place.

Slippery: I want her.

Chief: What? You want to play me in a game of chance?

Slippery: She's worth more than that. I will give you all that I own. For I too, am a chief. You may have my entire tribe—all the horses, all the cattle, all our pelts . . . if I may have her as my wife.

Chief: She's yours.

Slippery: Only if she will have me.

Curves: Yes! I mean, of course!

Chief: I do not understand.

Slippery: Our Heavenly Father has this message for you: How much I have given for her, He will give even more for you.

Slippery When Wet and Dangerous Curves leave the camp.

21

THE YANKEE HILLBILLIES

THEME
God's
Providence

PROPS AND NECESSITIES

☆ Hillbilly costumes
☆ 2 Cabin-like structures
☆ Cane
☆ Paper
☆ Pen

CAST

☆ Essie
☆ Paw
☆ Maw
☆ Governor Beauregard
☆ Intern
☆ Shawnessy

Essie runs onstage.

Essie: Mom! Dad! Mom—I mean, Maw! Paw! Come on outch'ere!

Maw and Paw enter from stage right.

Paw: Hey Essie! Whatchu' hollerin' 'bout?

Maw: I ain't seen you this excited since the Piggly Wiggly had that sale on boiled peanuts.

Essie: I won! I won the beauty pageant!

Maw: *(Drops hillbilly accent.)* Really? Congratulations, honey!

Paw: *(No hillbilly accent.)* That's wonderful, dear!

Essie: I smiled, I waved, I cat-walked, and I won!

Maw: Oh honey, we're so proud of you! What did you win? *(Clears throat, returns to hill-*

billy accent.) What's that mean ya' got comin' to ya'?

Essie: I get to meet the gov'ner!

Paw: The governor? Of this here state?

Essie: Well, no, not exactly. I'm gonna meet the gov'ner of Ar-Kansas!

Paw: Ar-Kansas? Why? What's wrong with the gov'ner of Georgia?

Maw: Paw, if you're gonna say it, say it right.

Paw: Georgia.

Maw: Jow-juh.

Paw: Gee-or-juh.

Maw: Jow-juh.

Paw: That's what I done said.

Maw: If you be wantin' any grits tonight you best get it through your thick skull! Jow-juh!

Paw: Jow-juh! But it don't matter none anyway. Essie is gonna meet the gov-'ner of Ar-Kansas.

Essie: Yep—tomorrow! And I get to take "two guests of my choice!"

Maw: So . . . who are ya' thinkin' about takin' witch'a?

Essie: Well . . . I was thinkin' 'bout takin' Billy Ray Cyrus and John Michael Montgomery.

Paw: What? Those two little pole wags?

Essie: Naw, I's just foolin' 'bout. I'm takin' the two of you, of course!

Paw: Yee-haw! I'm gonna go clean up my uat, buy me a new flannel shirt, and shine my boots!

Paw runs off stage right.

Maw: Oh, this means the world to your Paw. You just watch him get all gussied up. Wait—what am I saying? I'm gonna be meetin' the gov'ner too! What am I gonna wear? Oh, I gotta go do my hair!

Maw runs off stage right.

Essie: Aw, Maw, Paw, God bless ya'!

Essie follows her parents offstage. Governor Beauregard and his intern enter from stage left.

Intern: Governor Beauregard, the people are wonderin' what you got goin' on in your head with regards to the bull weevils that are—

Governor: When's lunch? I sho' is hungry.

Intern: But you just inhaled an entire—

Governor: *(Interrupting.)* I didn't inhale.

Essie enters from stage right, followed by Maw and Paw.

Intern: Sir, though I reckon you might still be hungry—

Governor: *(Interrupting; noticing Essie.)* Whoa, whoa, whoa. Who's that?

Intern: Essie McGovernflintock. She's the winner of the Miss Winn-Dixie Beauty Pageant.

Governor: Well, she ain't hard to look at, that's fo' sho'. Bring her on over here.

The intern goes over to Essie, Maw, and Paw.

Intern: Essie McGovernflintock? The governor will see you now.

Essie and the intern return to the governor.

Essie: It sho' is an honor and a privilege, sir.

Governor: Well, you're finer than a bouquet of dandelions on Sunday mornin', if you don't mind me sayin'.

Essie: *(Embarrassed.)* Awww . . .

Paw: *(To Maw.)* Did you hear that? Did you hear what he said to her? Jist who does he think he is?

Maw: Hush.

Governor: How would you like to work for me? As say, my intern?

Intern: Sir, you already have an intern.

Governor: Really? Who?

Intern: Me, sir.

Governor: Ah, yes indeed. Alright, how about a wife. Do I have one of those?

Intern: No, sir.

Governor: Essie McGovernflintock, how would you like to be my wife?

Essie: I dunno, sir. I've got class on Monday.

Governor: *Pleeeeeease?*

Essie: Aw, okay.

Paw: No! I won't have it! Who do you think you are, with your shirt buttoned down the middle, your car that still works with inflated tires, and your hair parted in the middle slicked down with Dapper Dan Easy Grease, Mister "I Brush My Teeth Three Times a Day?"

Governor: As a token of my gratitude for bringin' my wife into my life, I'd like to give ya'll this little cabin.

Maw: I always cry at weddin's.

Paw: That was *already* our cabin!

Essie and the governor exit stage left. Maw and Paw exit stage right.
The intern follows Essie and the governor. Shawnessy enters stage left.

Shawnessy: (*Singing to the tune of "The Beverly Hillbillies" theme song.*)
Before you know, Essie is a millionaire.
Kinfolk say "Ess' move away from there!"
They say "Ar-Kansas is the place you oughta be!"
So she packed up her goods and moved to Beverly.
Trailer Park, that is. Swimmin' holes. Lil' Rock.

Shawnessy exits the direction whence he came. Maw and Paw enter stage right .

Paw: (*Without hillbilly accent.*) I just don't like him, that's all.

Maw: (*No accent.*) Oh, he's nice enough. He reminds me of you when you were his age.

Paw: That's what I don't like about him!

The intern comes out of the governor's cabin.

Intern: Mister and Misses McGovernflintock, the governor is havin' a shindig and would like to invite the two of you's.

Paw: Well, thank-you.

Maw: We'd love to come.

Intern: Alright, would you—wait a minute! Where'd yer accents go?

Paw: What accents?

Maw: Oh, we're not really from down here.

Intern: Ar-Kansas, ya mean?

Maw: We're not from the South.

Intern: Yer Yanks?

Maw and Paw nod.

Paw: From New Jersey.

Intern: *New Jersey?* The governor of our fair state just married a Yankee spawn of-of-of *New Jersey?*

Maw: *(Smiling with pride.)* She won Little Miss Trenton just three years ago.

Paw: Oh, hey, we'd better get back inside. The Nets game is starting.

Maw and Paw retreat stage right.

Intern: I can't . . . I can't believe this! I've gotta tell the governor!

The governor enters stage left.

Governor: So, did the McGovernflintocks say they'd come to my right-fine shindig?

Intern: Sir, may I ask you a question?

Governor: That's one. Wanna ask me another one?

Intern: Sir, do you like the way things are?

Governor: Well, I know there need to be some changes. The machines downstairs don't take my beat-up dollar bills, and I like candy. We need ta pass a law for free candy! Or maybe fer—

Intern: No, sir, that's not what I'm talkin' about. I mean here. In Ar-Kansas.

Governor: Well we couldn't pass a law for free candy just in Little Rock. That wouldn't hardly be—.

Intern: So you think things should stay the same.

Governor: No they shouldn't. I want candy!

Intern: But we should try to get rid of any evil influence that might—

Governor: *(Interrupting.)* Candy machine operators!

Intern: Yes! No! I mean . . . Wait a second . . . *(A wicked grin spreads across the intern's face.)* Yeah . . . Sir, do you know who invented those candy machines?

Governor: Willy Wonka?

Intern: And who plays Willy Wonka?

Governor: Some weirdo from Hollywood?

Intern: And where is Hollywood?

Governor: Californy!

Intern: And is Californy part of the South?

Governor: I don't rightly think so . . .

Intern: *(Growing passionate.)* No, it's the North!

Governor: I thought it was the West . . .

Intern: Sir, anyplace that isn't part of the South is part of the North! And we don't need any Northerners running around here fowling up our candy machines. Send them back to where they came from! *(Pulls out a piece of paper.)* Sir, sign this and send those carpet-baggers packin'!

Governor: That's right! Stealin' my candy. Ya' can't do that and get away with it!

The governor signs the paper.

Intern: Everything if fine now, sir. Everything will be (smiling wickedly) "taken care of."

The governor exits to his cabin; the intern exits stage left.
Maw and Paw come racing out of their cabin.

Maw: Essie!

Paw: Essie!

Maw: Come quick!

Essie races out of her cabin.

Essie: What? What is it?

Maw: Did you hear?

Paw:	The governor just passed a law that says all us "Northern folk" are gonna be rounded up and put down!
Maw:	You've gotta do something, Essie!
Essie:	What can I do? I'm just a girl. I mean . . .
Paw:	It's up to you, Essie. You have to go talk to him.
Essie:	But no one's allowed in his cabin during nap time. Do you know what happens to people who interrupt the governor's nap time?
Paw:	But you're our only hope, Essie!
Essie:	(Pauses.) Alright. I'll do it. But everyone needs to pray first. Come on!

The three of them kneel in prayer, then Maw and Paw exit. Essie approaches the governor, who is asleep inside his cabin. Essie slowly approaches. As she reaches the cabin and knocks, the governor suddenly wakes up and points his cane at her.

Governor:	Who's that?
Essie:	It's me.
Governor:	Oh. (Lowers cane.) Whatchu' want?
Essie:	(No accent.) Well, husband of mine, you passed a law today that says I'm gonna soon face my doom.
Governor:	No I didn't. It says all those good for nothin' Northerners are 'sposed to be rounded up. You're not—wait, where's your accent?
Essie:	Oh, Jimmy-Jack, my name isn't really Essie. It's Esther. And I'm from New Jersey. That's very north of here and . . . my parents and I moved down here when I was very little and we just wanted to fit in so we started saying "ya'll" instead of "you guys" and stuff like that.
Governor:	Let me get this straight. You all is from the North?
Essie:	Yo.
Governor:	And you steal people's candy?

Essie: *(Uncertainly.)* No . . .

Governor: Northerners won't sell us candy 'cause we got beat-up dollar bills!

Essie: What? That's not true.

Governor: It's not? Intern!

The intern enters, running, from stage left.

Intern: Yes, sir?

Governor: Did you lie to me?

Intern: Today, you mean?

Governor: About Northerners?

Intern: *(Sheepishly.)* Maybe a little bit.

Governor: I do not tolerate liars. You are banished to . . . New Jersey!

Intern: *Nnnnnnnnoooooooooooo!*

The intern faints.

Essie: Wow! So what did we learn from all this?

Governor: Always use quarters when you want a Kit-Kat.

Essie: That's it? That's what you learned? You didn't learn anything about how you can't judge someone because of where they're from? Or that one person can make a difference? Or that God has big plans for each of us and will give us talents to take us there?

Governor: I knew that.

Essie: *(To audience.)* And now you do too.

Essie and the governor exit.

22

AND THERE WAS WAR

THEME
The Great Controversy

PROPS AND NECESSITIES

☆ "Heavenly" costumes
☆ Chair
☆ Dark make-up
☆ Black costume
☆ Punk clothes
☆ Seductive female clothes

CAST

☆ Michael
☆ Lucifer
☆ Gabriel
☆ Serenity
☆ Orion
☆ Faith
☆ Azrael
☆ Loki

SCENE 1

All stage lights are off. A chair is set at stage right. Michael enters from stage left, with Lucifer following close behind. All are dressed in white.

Michael: Let there be light!

All stage lights flip on. Michael laughs.

Michael: I love doing that.

Lucifer laughs.

Lucifer: Something tells me there's more where that came from!

Michael laughs, becoming very excited. He uses his entire body to explain what he's talking about.

Michael: I know it's not much to look at right now, but just you wait. By the end of the week, it will be amazing. I'm going to put the garden in right over there, with all sorts of fruits and veggies and animals! All kinds of animals! I'm going to get some water flowing through here . . .

Lucifer: You've really thought this one through.

Michael: I *always* think them through.

Lucifer: But this isn't your typical "fixer-upper," is it? This one's special, isn't?

Michael: *(Thoughtfully.)* Yes, it is.

Lucifer: I could tell. I've watched You as You've tackled project after project. You've been doing this for eons! But I've never quite seen that twinkle in your eye. What's so special about this one?

Michael: It's—

Lucifer: *(Interrupting.)* It's for me, isn't it?

Michael: What?

Lucifer: My own little place to call my own. A place where I can truly shine. You're passing the mantle on to me for my years of dedicated service. You're finally going to let this little flame be a raging fire.

Michael is quite disturbed by this speech.

Michael: No, not at all. What makes this place so special is who is going to live here. I'm going to make them in my image.

Lucifer: What?

Michael: Don't get me wrong. You're a strong leader, but only under and through me.

Lucifer: I-I'm not going to have my own kingdom? Ever?

Michael: Lucifer . . . you're not God.

A silent moment.

Michael: I'm going to stay here a while. You going back?

| Lucifer: | (*Distracted.*) Yes. |

Michael exits stage left and Lucifer sits down in the chair at stage right.

SCENE 2

Lucifer is sulking in the chair. Allow time for Lucifer to wallow in his anger, jealousy, and frustration. Gabriel enters from stage left.

Gabriel:	Hey, Bright Angel. You call this meeting?
Lucifer:	(*Glaring.*) Don't call me that.
Gabriel:	Shouldn't Michael be here for this?
Lucifer:	(*Snaps.*) No. He can't be here for this.
Gabriel:	(*Joking.*) Why? Are we throwing Him some kind of surprise party?

Lucifer is taken aback but actually likes the comparison.

Lucifer:	Actually, yes. Exactly. A "surprise party."
Gabriel:	(*Surprised.*) Oh.
Lucifer:	Where is everybody?
Gabriel:	They're—
Lucifer:	(*Interrupting.*) Why don't you go round them up? Make yourself useful for once.

Gabriel, taken aback and confused, exits stage right.

| Lucifer: | (*To himself.*) So lazy. |

Serenity enters from stage left. She slowly dances her way across stage.

| Serenity: | Lucifer, do you want to tell me what's going on? |
| Lucifer: | Serenity, you are the most—dare I say it?—"cunning" of all the angels. |

Serenity: *(Teasing.)* Don't change the subject.

Charity enters from stage right.

Lucifer: Everyone will find out soon enough.

Serenity gives Charity a nod.

Serenity: Welcome, Charity.

Charity is uneasy. She doesn't like the idea of going behind Michael's back like this.

Charity: Is Michael back yet?

Lucifer: No. We're no longer "priority number one" with Him. He finds His new little pet project more important.

Charity: What?

Lucifer: You can't tell me you haven't seen it, Charity. How fondly and how excitedly He talks about it. He spends so much time down there He hardly has time for us anymore.

Serenity: That's not true . . .

Lucifer: It might as well be! He's been down there for four days now, and He hasn't even created "them" yet! You see how much time He's spent on just creating a piece of dirt they can live on! What's going to happen at the end of the week and He creates "them" in His image? He's going to want to spend every waking minute with them and you know it. That'll leaving us alone up here to run His kingdom while He's off romping with . . . with . . . "them!"

Charity is shocked. Serenity is silent as she considers Lucifer's words..

Charity: Where is this coming from?

Lucifer: Too timid to face the truth?

One at a time, the other angels enter: Orion from stage left,
Faith from stage right, Azrael from stage right and Gabriel from stage left.

Orion: Alright, we're all here.

Gabriel: I trust you have a good reason for breaking protocol. Only the Godhead may call a meeting of the Seraphim.

Lucifer walks about stage like a commanding officer before his troops.

Lucifer: The strongest of the strong! The mightiest of the mighty! The elite. The few, the proud, the Seraphim. We are God's chosen leaders.

Orion: We know we are the Seraphim. What's this meeting about?

Lucifer: Impatience is a virtue I can handle. Gets the job done quicker, doesn't it? Fine. No formalities. No chit-chat. No further adieu. Let me put it on the proverbial "bottom shelf": I believe Michael's priorities have shifted.

No one really knows how to take this statement.
Everyone stares at Lucifer as if he has lost his mind.

Azrael: Meaning . . . ?

Lucifer: *(Mumbling.)* Six heads and not a brain among them. Do you not see? We've been following Him so blindly for so long that we don't understand a challenge when we hear one! Let me spell it out: Michael, His Royal One-ness, does not love us the way He used to!

Gabriel: I'm not going to stay here and listen to this.

Gabriel exits stage left.

Faith: What are you trying to do? Are you trying to declare war on the throne? Michael has proved to us time after time that the only word we could ever use to describe Him is "love."

Lucifer: *(Sacastically.)* Love. Do you call this love? He's been so busy with His little genesis project that He hardly has time for us anymore.

Faith: That's a lie!

Lucifer: Truth is in the eye of the beholder.

Charity: Lucifer, that's not true . . . is it?

Lucifer: Depends on your point of view.

Azrael: Tell us your point of view, Lucifer.

Lucifer: You see how he holds me back. He's always creating planets, and He'll never let me be a part of it. He's afraid of me.

Charity: If He's not, suddenly I am.

Lucifer: He knows how much better I'd be at it! Just look at me! I'm leadership material, and He knows it!

Faith: Of course He knows it. He created you!

Serenity: And you're head of the choir.

Lucifer: I'm His right-hand man! You hear how He's always rambling about how "being trusted with small things will lead to being trusted with big things."

Serenity: *(As if she's figured it out.)* So this *would* be the next logical step . . .

Lucifer: One planet! That's all I've ever asked for! Just one! Countless times I've fallen on my knees, pleading and begging for this one request to be granted, only to be denied every time!

Faith: Well maybe—

Lucifer: *(Interrupting.)* But what absolute power requires itself to be bestowed? If He has the power to give, can He not also take away? I'd be nothing more than His puppet! If I truly want the power that I deserve, then I must take it!

A silent beat and then everyone begins yelling at Lucifer at the same time. These parts may be ad-libbed, but the spirit of these characters should remain the same.

Orion: You're talking like you're on the same level as Michael! He's your Creator! He gives you everything you have, everything you need!

Faith: You can't do this, Lucifer. He loves you so much! If you go through with this, you would break His heart!

Serenity: He's so much more powerful than you! He could blot you out of existence with a snap of the finger!

Azrael: You can't take on the Throne! You're just one man! Now's not the time!

Charity: Have you actually stopped and thought about what you've been saying? You're out of your mind! Are you just making this up as you go?

Lucifer holds his hands up to silence them, laughing. Everyone quiets down.

Lucifer: Don't worry my friends. This is merely the beginning.

Lucifer exits stage right. In stunned silence, everyone watches him leave. Then, one by one, each angel leaves, exiting stage left. Serenity is the last to leave.

SCENE 3

Michael slowly enters from stage left. As He crosses center stage, Gabriel quickly catches up to Him from stage left.

Gabriel: Michael! My Lord Michael!

Michael: Gabriel.

Gabriel: You're back none too soon. Lucifer is—

Michael: *(Interrupting.)* I know.

Gabriel: What are You going to do?

Michael: What *can* I do?

Gabriel: *(Stunned.)* What do you mean? It's not like You're not all-powerful! We must stop this! We can't let Lucifer spread his lies! He's got to be stopped.

Michael: What would you have me do?

Gabriel: You speak and solar systems come into existence. Perfectly, delicately balanced ecosystems are derived from just one of Your thoughts. If You can create, can You not "un-create?"

It pains Michael to even hear this, let alone imagine it.

Gabriel: If there is life, there must be an absence of life. Could you not—

Michael: (*Interrupting*) No.

Gabriel: But why not?

Michael: As loyal as your intentions are, if I were to do what you're asking of Me, I would only be proving his point. I would be telling all the worlds that I require their slavery. I am not a God of slaves. I am one of love and freedom. Everyone: you, the angels, and all the worlds must have the freedom to choose. Even Lucifer must choose. Though this will only get worse before it gets better, perhaps I can prove my love to all, once and for all, by letting Lucifer live. Though he seeks only to destroy Me and all that I've created, I will let him live. I could erase both his memory and his very existence and his memory. But I cannot—I will not—because I love him.

A deep, profound silence ensues. Gabriel, humbled, ventures forward with a question.

Gabriel: So what happens next?

Michael: Sin cannot live in My presence. It must be expelled. But it is not a sin to be tempted. All will be tempted. Even now, Lucifer is tempting himself. You, I, and all that are will be tempted. We must save them all. (*Pauses.*) Now go. Warn them.

Gabriel turns to exit stage left and sees Lucifer enter. Dark circles are under his eyes.

Gabriel: Speaking of sin . . .

Lucifer: Watch your mouth Pretty Boy. Get outta here. This is between me and Him.

Michael nods His consent and Gabriel exits stage left.

Michael: What is it, Lucifer?

Lucifer: (*Sarcastically.*) You tell me, O Great Omniscient One. (*Pause.*) Alright then, I suppose you could say I'm "calling you out."

Michael: On what?

Lucifer: Don't patronize me! You know what!

Michael: How have I wronged you? What grievous mistake did I commit to cause this uprising?

Lucifer: Perhaps creating me perfect was your first mistake. Just look at me! I'm bold, I'm beautiful, I'm decisive, I'm intelligent—a natural leader. And You have me waste it all as I sit idly by Your side.

Michael: We hardly have an idle moment.

Lucifer: I want command! Control!

Michael: I Am the only Being to whom you answer.

Lucifer: That's One too many.

Michael looks at Lucifer, reading his every thought and body movement.

Michael: Having convinced yourself that I've slighted you, you're bringing war to Heaven?

Lucifer: Until Your throne is mine.

Michael sighs. It breaks His heart to think of the consequences.

Michael: Why?

Lucifer: You're the One whose priorities have suddenly shifted.

Michael: I have never stopped loving you.

Lucifer: Save Your "love" for Your new pets. You give love a bad name. *(Turns to leave.)* I'll see You on the battlefield.

Lucifer exits stage left. Michael exits stage right.

<u>SCENE 4</u>

Loki enters from stage right as Azrael enters from stage left. Azrael has dark circles under his eyes.

Loki: Can you believe this? Civil war, here in heaven!

Azrael: Mind-boggling, to be sure. Which side do you support?

Loki: I'm not getting involved.

Azrael: What?

Loki: This is between Lucifer and Michael. When it's over, we'll get on with life.

Azrael: It's not that way. You have to choose one side or the other.

Loki: Why? Why do I have to choose a side? As soon as I take a side, I'll be attacked by the other! Thanks, but no thanks. I'll just sit here, mind my own business, and hope to be notified when the dust settles.

Azrael: So . . . you don't believe Michael enough to defend Him, and you don't have enough proof to back up Lucifer.

Loki: I shouldn't have to explain myself to you! If I don't want to get involved, I don't want to get involved!

Lucifer enters from stage left.

Lucifer: Azrael, friend, ease up. If he doesn't want to fight, so be it. It's better for him not to fight than to fight against us, though your lack of faith is both noted and disturbing.

Lucifer smiles. It's not a friendly smile but it's not an evil one either. It's a smile of something cooking in the back of his head.

Lucifer: Just relax. Take it easy. Don't make any rash decisions. Whenever you feel ready, come see me and we'll talk—no strings attached.

Loki, feeling better and leaning toward Lucifer's side more than ever, exits stage right.

Azrael: What's up with that? Why'd you let him go?

Lucifer: His indecisiveness is his vote. When it comes to Michael, you're either for Him or against Him. If Loki will not align himself with Michael, he has no other choice but to align with us.

Azrael: I still don't get it.

Lucifer:	It's the great "rule of opposites." Whatever doesn't work for Him works for me, and vice versa. Now get outta here. I've got someone to talk to.
Azrael:	Who?

To answer the question, Lucifer points to stage left as Charity and Serenity enter. Azrael understands and exits stage right. Lucifer flashes a dazzling smile.

Lucifer:	I was wondering when I'd see you again. You really are angelic beings.
Charity:	That would make sense, being as we are angels.

Lucifer puts his arms around them. Serenity doesn't even react. Charity is less "at home" in Lucifer's arms.

Lucifer:	That's not how I meant it. Don't you think that the two of you belong by the side of the most powerful being in all creation?

Charity pulls away from Lucifer, though Serenity doesn't. Lucifer immediately ignores Charity and turns to Serenity, "checking her out."

Charity:	I have nothing to say to you and I don't want to hear anything you have to say to me.

Lucifer doesn't even take his eyes off Serenity.

Lucifer:	Fine. Whatever. I don't care. Leave.

Charity exits stage left. Lucifer doesn't care. He smiles at Serenity.

Lucifer:	(*To Serenity.*) You're the one I wanted anyway.
Serenity:	Me?
Lucifer:	You question me? Of course you do. You are the only one in existence that even comes close to rivaling me. And we weren't made for this. We were made to be more. You *can* feel it, can't you? All that pent up passion. It's become your prison. Break free! Follow me and we'll make all our dreams come true. Anything! Everything! We'll rule, just the two of us, doing whatever we want.
Serenity:	But what about Michael?

Lucifer: Who needs Him? We've got each other. I mean, that's what friends are for, right?

Serenity is hesitant. She wants to believe Lucifer, but that would mean turning her back on Michael. Lucifer sees this.

Lucifer: I've always been there for you. And have I ever asked you to change a single thing about you? No! Even now, all I'm asking you to do is to stop denying yourself what you really want and need!

Serenity smiles. She is touched by Lucifer's words.
Putting her arm around him, the two exit stage right.

<u>SCENE 5</u>

Loki enters from stage right. He has dark circles under his eyes. Michael enters from stage left. Loki turns around, not wanting a confrontation. Lucifer enters from stage right. Still trying to avoid confrontation, Loki about-faces quickly and finds himself someplace he doesn't want to be. He panics and scurries off stage right as Orion enters from stage right.

Orion: And just what was *that* all about?

Lucifer: He's just trying to stay out of trouble.

Orion: Trouble *you* caused. All this confusion, all this hurt and heartache, is because of you!

Orion turns to Michael pleadingly.

Orion: Isn't that true? You didn't have anything to do with all this, did You?

Michael: You know Me well. Have I ever done anything to confuse you?

Orion: No.

Michael: Have I ever done anything to hurt you?

Orion: No.

Michael: Have I ever done anything, even just once, that has caused you heartache?

Orion: No.

Michael:	You know Me. You know I don't stand for this. I could never start anything like this.
Lucifer:	How can You stand there and act like You had nothing to do with any of this? If You're "Creator of all," should You not be ultimately held accountable for the actions of Your creations?
Michael:	*(With power and resolution.)* I Am.
Lucifer:	*(Taken aback.)* What did you say?
Orion:	*(Confused.)* What does that mean?

Faith enters from stage left.

Faith:	You know precisely what that means! While Lucifer can only blame others, Michael takes full responsibility for His actions. Orion, you have to stay strong. Michael's never led us astray before. You can trust Him.
Lucifer:	No!
Orion:	No, Lucifer! I've heard enough from you.

Orion and Faith exit stage left.

Lucifer:	Why are you doing this to me? We used to be best friends, but now . . . now I can't even stand to be in Your presence! Nothing made me happier than being with You, doing Your will. What have You done to me? Every shred of laughter is gone. Now . . . all I want . . . is You . . . on Your knees, begging for mercy and forgiveness from me! I want Your blood and I want Your soul and I want them both now!

Michael regards Lucifer for a moment.

Michael:	*(Softly.)* All I ever wanted—
Lucifer:	*(Interrupting.)* I'm tired of hearing what You want! It's always about You, You, You! But no longer!

Lucifer rips off his white robe, revealing a black costume.

Lucifer:	From now on, I'm only worrying about two things: myself and my war

against You.

Loki, Azrael, and Serenity enter from stage right.

Lucifer: We're leaving this sham You call "heaven" and taking the battle with us.

Azrael: *(To Michael.)* We'll tell them all about this little charade You're playing with them.

Azrael takes off his white robe, revealing punk clothes.

Serenity: We'll show them true freedom.

Serenity takes off her white robe, revealing her seductive get-up.

Loki: Why are You making us leave? What did we ever do to You?

Loki takes off his white robe, revealing alcoholic beverage T-shirt and jeans.

Michael: No. Don't. You don't have to—

Azrael: *(Interrupting.)* Save it. It's too late.

Azrael leads Loki and Serenity off stage left.

Lucifer: And there You have it. You know my resolve. I will not fail; I will not quit until Your throne is mine!

A sudden thought strikes Lucifer.

Lucifer: But why postpone the victory when I can have it now?

Michael puts up His hand, stopping Lucifer without touching him. Gabriel rushes out from stage right and grabs Lucifer, holding his arms behind his back. Lucifer struggles but cannot escape.

Michael: And you know my resolve, Satan. Wherever you try to go, I will be three steps ahead of you. Even after you've left My presence, I will still be there, giving hope to those from whom you steal it; loving those whom you pervert; trusting and keeping those whom you persecute. They will know Me and know My love. If you must have a war, so be it. But you will not overtake us.

Michael and Lucifer stare into each other's eyes.

Michael: Take him away.

Gabriel drags the squirming Lucifer off stage left. Michael, brokenhearted,
takes center stage. He rubs his forehead. Gabriel reenters, and Michael speaks again.

Michael: The fight begun today will rage on and on, but it will not change. The choices made today will have to be made day in, day out, until I end this. We must save as many as We can.

23

AFTER THE DEMONS

THEME
Unconditional
Acceptance

PROPS AND NECESSITIES

☆ Table
☆ Chairs
☆ Items on table
(see script)

CAST

☆ Elizabeth
☆ Samantha
☆ Asher
☆ Father
☆ Darren

Scene 1

The setting is a cemetery. Elizabeth enters cautiously, looking this way and that, making sure the coast is clear. Turning back in the direction from which she came, she calls out.

Elizabeth: *(Sarcastically.)* C'mon, Sam! The coast is clear!

Samantha timidly enters. She glances around.

Samantha: Are you sure? I've heard some really scary stuff about this place, like—

Elizabeth: *(Interrupts.)* It's just a cemetery! Grassy knolls and tall stones! Besides, you know as well as I do there is no such thing as ghouls, ghosts, and goblins!

Samantha: Well, yeah, but Daddy says that demons like to live here and, well, what if he's right? W-we could *die!*

Elizabeth: Samantha, what do we have to be scared of? It's broad daylight! Isn't there a rule about demons lurking only at night? Besides, they can hurt you only if you let them. And they can take control of you only if you let them.

When Elizabeth says "It's broad daylight," Asher enters on all fours, like an ape. His clothes are old and torn. He looks at the girls curiously, cocking his head this way and that. Samantha sees him immediately and freaks out, although she doesn't say anything (she's been rendered speechless). Elizabeth's back is to Asher.

Elizabeth: What?

Samantha: Th-th-there's some *thing* behind you!

Elizabeth: What did you say?

Samantha: It . . . OK, on the count of three we'll run back the same way we came. The gate is still open. We can make it.

Elizabeth: What are you talking about?

Asher has a speech impediment.

Asher: Hello!

Samantha and Elizabeth scream. Elizabeth spins around. Asher jumps back defensively.

Samantha: It can talk! We're gonna die!

With another scream, Samantha crumples to the floor in a faint. Elizabeth grabs Samantha's arm, as if to pick her up.

Elizabeth: Samantha! Get up! This is no time for—get up!

Asher, still on all fours, slowly approaches.

Elizabeth: (*To Asher.*) Heh, heh . . . nice . . . man—thing . . . stay right there . . . stay . . . stay!

Asher sits back into a crouch, resting his arms on his knees. He is obviously disturbed at the sight of the fallen Samantha.

Asher: Is she gonna be OK?

Elizabeth turns from Samantha to Asher.

Elizabeth: What?

Asher leans forward onto his fists and slowly approaches.

Asher: I didn't mean to hurt her! It was an accident, honest! Is she gonna be OK?

Elizabeth was not expecting this and does not know how to answer.

Elizabeth: Well, I, uh, think so . . .

Asher crawls closer, and Elizabeth takes a step back. Asher places his ear close to Samantha's mouth and nose. Leaning back, he smiles.

Asher: She's breathing! *(Gives a thumbs up.)* Yesss!

Elizabeth: You're not at all evil, are you? What, I mean, *who* are you?

Asher: Asher. That's my name, Asher.

Elizabeth: Asher?

Asher: Yep, Asher. That's what my parents named me, Asher.

Elizabeth: What are you doing out here?

Asher: I live out here.

Elizabeth laughs.

Elizabeth: You live here? C'mon, really. What are you doing here in the cemetery?

Asher: I'm all by myself. Here in the cemetery. I live here. This my home. Me and the dead folks. *(Asher smiles.)*

Elizabeth: What? Wh-why would you live out *here?*

Asher: Nobody likes me, everybody hates me.

Elizabeth:	Why would anyone hate you?

Elizabeth looks down at Samantha and remembers what just happened. She laughs nervously.

Elizabeth:	Don't you have any friends or family?
Asher:	Nobody likes me, everybody hates me. Except Legion. But Legion became mean, took over. They made me do things and say things I didn't want to say and that made people hate me more. So now I've lived here for . . . what's it been, 10 years? Ten years. Yep, 10.
Elizabeth:	*Ten years?*
Asher:	Yep! Ever since Jesus said, "Legion, go get in them pigs!" And they did! Legion left me alone, but everyone's still scared of me.
Elizabeth:	But you *can't* live out here! It's just not right!
Asher:	Where else can I live? That girl right there screamed and fainted when she looked at me!

Asher points to Samantha.

Elizabeth:	You . . . you could, well . . .

Elizabeth turns aside and speaks to herself.

Elizabeth:	We have that extra room upstairs . . . No, Daddy would have a fit; he wouldn't hear of it! But . . . I can't just leave him here . . .

Samantha moans and stirs slightly.

Asher:	Uh-oh—she's waking up.

Elizabeth falls to her knees beside her sister.

Elizabeth:	Samantha! Are you alright?

Samantha slowly sits up, groaning.

Samantha:	Oh . . . Elizabeth! I had the strangest dream! I dreamed that we were walking home from the market, and that we were running late, so we cut

through the cemetery, and this bizarre little man crawled up to us and . . .

Samantha sees Asher squatting there. She turns to Elizabeth, with dread
in her voice, she knows the answer before she even asks the question.

Samantha: It *was* a dream, wasn't it?

Elizabeth: No.

Samantha looks over at Asher, and it looks as though she's going to start crying.

Asher: Hey, it's OK . . .

Elizabeth helps Samantha to her feet.

Elizabeth: C'mon, we need to get home.

Samantha: And none too soon!

Samantha begins to exit, and Elizabeth turns to Asher.

Elizabeth: You follow us. We'll take you somewhere safe.

Samantha spins around.

Samantha: Excuse me?

Elizabeth: Asher is coming home with us. We can't just leave him here. Think about it. He's out here in the cold and . . . Oh, for cryin' out loud, he's living in a cemetery! That just isn't right! He deserves a house—a home—as much as the next person!

Samantha: Then let the next cemetery shortcut-taker give him a home!

Elizabeth: Asher is coming with us.

Samantha: But what about Father?

Elizabeth: I'll deal with Father. Now come on, it's getting late.

Samantha scurries off stage. Elizabeth turns and speaks to Asher.

Elizabeth: You coming?

Asher, on all fours, follows Elizabeth off stage.

Scene 2

A table is set with two chairs at just left of center stage. Dad enters and sits at the table. He waits there impatiently, constantly checking his watch and looking from his left to his right. Finally Darren enters. Darren is very proud and rather full of himself.

Father: Ah, Darren! Just the man I wanted to see!

Darren: Good day to you, Mr. Reubenson. What can I do for you?

Father gestures toward the other chair.

Father: Here, have a seat.

Darren holds up his hand.

Darren: Thanks, but no.

Father: Can I get you a refreshment?

Darren: No.

Father: Ah, well, then . . . Now, I know it's none of my business, but I couldn't help but notice how you are, uh, how do you say, a "bachelor."

Darren: Yes?

Father: Well, you're getting up there in your years. It won't be too much longer until you're 25!

Darren: Let's come to terms, Mr. Reubenson. You are not concerned about me being single. You're worried that your daughter Elizabeth will not be married. For if she is not married, how will you ever marry off Samantha who, well, let's admit it, is the one who got her mother's good looks.

Father: You have always had a way with words, Darren.

Darren: *(Proudly.)* So I've been told.

Father: Yes, well, maybe that is my concern. But I have every reason to be worried. Elizabeth is 18 years old! Most girls her age are already a mother! Some even have two children!

Darren: Ah yes, and you don't want to see fair Elizabeth become an old maid. *(Pauses.)* Well, what will you give me to marry her?

Father: *(Taken aback.)* I beg your pardon?

Darren: What will you give me? What will you pay me?

Father: I do believe that my daughter's hand in marriage is enough "payment" for you, Darren!

Darren: And what of the dowry? It is customary for the father of the bride to pay a handsome dowry for his daughter.

Father: Oh, that. Of course, of course. I am more than willing to pay the husband-to-be 10 hand-woven robes of his own color choice!

> *Darren throws his head back and laughs.*

Darren: You can't be serious!

Father: Now Darren, I'm struggling to keep my business going. I can't afford to give away even one single, simple robe, let alone 10! Some of us aren't as blessed as others . . .

Darren: Too true, too true. I really do pity those less fortunate than I . . . which would be . . . everyone.

> *Darren laughs at his own joke, but Father just stares at him, smiling weakly. Samantha enters.*

Father: Ah, Samantha, you're back! Where's Elizabeth?

> *Samantha sees Darren and gets nervous, remembering Asher.*

Samantha: Uh, well, it's like this . . . What was the question?

Darren: *(Under his breath.)* Mother's good looks and father's dull mind . . .

Father: Where is your sister?

Samantha: Outside—almost inside—but still outside. Be right back!

Samantha spins around to rush out, but Elizabeth enters with Asher. Elizabeth sees Darren and her father and immediately turns to Asher, who's still on all fours. Everyone is silent. Asher slowly crawls into the open.

Darren: What, in the name of all that's good and plenty, is that?

Elizabeth: His name is Asher.

Father: I don't care if he followed you home—you can't keep him!

Samantha and Elizabeth grow excited.

Samantha: He didn't follow us home; we brought him home!

Elizabeth: He was living in the cemetery!

Samantha: What kind of life is that?

Elizabeth: He needs a home!

Samantha: And we have an extra room!

Elizabeth: He needs a family!

Samantha: You always wanted a son!

Elizabeth: He needs the respect, love, and dignity to which every human is entitled!

Samantha: Yeah!

Father and Darren are speechless. Asher just sits there, a little unsure of the whole situation. Darren snaps out of his daze. He approaches Asher and slowly walks around him.

Darren: How long did you live in the cemetery?

Asher: Ten years.

Darren: How can you *live* in a cemetery? I mean, what does a person *eat* when they live in a graveyard?

Asher: Whatever. Rats taste like chicken, by the way, only a bit gamier.

Father: *What?*

Elizabeth: Well think about it! He was living there and was possessed by demons! He was doing stuff he didn't want to do!

Samantha: Yeah! It's not like he could just go to the refrigerator and pull out some leftovers!

*Dad stands up and, keeping his eyes on Asher, approaches him. He doesn't
say a word as he now cautiously walks a slow circle around Asher. Kneeling down,
he looks into Asher's eyes. Asher stares back at the father questioningly.*

Father: You're a good man, Asher. I can see it. You may stay in my house—for now.

Darren: Mr. Reubenson, you can't be serious! This *thing* could—

Father stands up and faces Darren with such abruptness that the latter instantly stops talking,

Father: Darren, I respect you and your opinion. But do not forget your place. While you stand under my roof, you will respect my decisions and will not question my authority.

Samantha: Yeah, and then some!

Darren looks at each of the people in the room, shocked, surprised, and angry.

Darren: Fine! But don't say I didn't warn you! Mark my words, nothing good will come of this!

Darren storms out. Father, Elizabeth, and Samantha all sigh.

Father: Asher, you'll have to forgive Darren for his exceptionally large mouth. He's living proof that the larger one's mouth gets, the harder it is to control.

Elizabeth: His father is the high priest, and his son thinks that he can do no wrong.

Samantha: He's just full of himself, that's all.

Asher: I've heard worse.

Elizabeth:	Well, let's get you cleaned up.

Samantha plugs her nose.

Samantha:	Yes, and a new change of clothes!
Father:	Yes, indeed. Follow us, Asher.

Father, Samantha, and Elizabeth walk off, and Asher follows.

Scene 3

Asher enters, still on all fours still, but now he's wearing new clothes.
He sports an untucked, button-down shirt and khakis but no shoes.
Asher pulls back a chair from the table and squats on it. He reaches for an
apple from a bowl in the middle of the table just as Samantha enters, humming.

Samantha:	Good morning, Asher! You're certainly up early.
Asher:	Couldn't sleep.
Samantha:	Oh? Up all night?
Asher:	Bed too soft. I need a good rock.

Samantha is a little confused at this thought, but dismisses it.

Samantha:	Oh. Well, we'll figure something out for you. So what do you want to do today? Have any plans? *(Pauses.)* What am I asking you that for—you lived in a cemetery! What kind of plans could you have? Elizabeth and I have to see to father's store; he left early this morning for Jerusalem. Passover, you know? He'll be back Monday night. You can hang out with us, if you want.
Asher:	I want to go outside!
Samantha:	We can do that in a little bit.

Asher smiles happily and takes a bite out of the apple. Samantha continues speaking.

Samantha:	Asher, do you think I'm pretty?

*Asher almost chokes on his apple. He looks at
Samantha, embarrassed and searching for words.*

Asher: Well, I, uh, "pretty" is . . . What?

Samantha laughs and sits down beside Asher.

Samantha: Forget I asked.

Asher looks at Samantha, studying her.

Asher: What do *you* think?

Samantha: What does it matter what I think? I'm just the "dumb little sister." What I think doesn't count. What I want doesn't matter. I can't do anything without my sister breathing down my neck. When I voice my opinion, it just gets ignored. Oh, but not Elizabeth! When she talks, all of earth waits in eager expectation! It's so unfair. The only way I can get attention is by messing up and being stupid.

Asher: You're not stupid. You're not even a messer-upper. You're booty-ful.

Samantha smiles at Asher and ruffles his hair.

Samantha: Thanks, Asher. You're sweet. And if you were any other man, I'd be deeply touched. But since all you really have to compare me with is decaying bodies, well, it loses some of the magic.

Asher: No, I'm not comparing you to dead people. I look at a little flower or a bird in the sky, or a big sunset. They're very pretty. God made them. God made you too. God doesn't make ugly stuff.

*Samantha looks at Asher with amazement. A small smile is on
her lips. Leaning over, she plants a small kiss on Asher's cheek.*

Samantha: Thanks, Asher. You keep that attitude and you'll go places. And speaking of going places, I'd better do just that. Tell Elizabeth, whenever she gets up, that I went into town to get the ingredients for the Passover bread. We're out of flour. See ya' later.

Asher: Bye.

Samantha exits. Asher smiles as he speaks to himself.

Asher: Samantha . . . kissed me. Me. She kissed me. I got kissed by a girl! And her name was Samantha! *(Asher's smile fades to a frown.)* But if she knew . . . she wouldn't kiss me. God never made ugly stuff . . . but *I'm* ugly. Nobody likes me, everybody hates me.

But she kissed me! Why? *(Pauses, then shouts.)* Who cares? I got my first kiss ever this very morning! I rock!

Elizabeth enters.

Elizabeth: Good morning, Asher!

Asher: I got kissed by a girl!

Elizabeth spins around and faces Asher, startled.

Elizabeth: *What?*

Asher realizes this was a tidbit of information that should not have been shared. He looks all around, as if searching for a way out of this conversation. Elizabeth continues.

Elizabeth: Did you say what I think you said?

Asher: Uh . . . I . . . um . . . well . . .

Elizabeth: It's all right, you're not in trouble.

Asher: Samantha kissed me.

Elizabeth: She did *what?*

Asher leaps off the chair and looks for a place to go.

Asher: Sorry! It'll never happen again! Never!

Elizabeth sighs and sits at the table.

Elizabeth: It's OK, Asher. It's not your fault. Samantha is just . . . well, she's just that way. She never changes. She always has 12 men following her, wherever she goes. She flirts with them like crazy. If I've told her once, I've told her a million times: she's asking for trouble by doing that! One of these days, some guy is going to take her seriously, and when she tries to avoid him, he'll . . . he'll hurt her . . .

Asher: Who would hurt Samantha?

Elizabeth: No one—yet. I'm just saying that the way guys pay attention to her, it's bound to happen. I mean, *all* the guys just fawn all over her. They always come by asking for her, they always bring her things, they always—

Asher: *(Interrupting.)* Why you jealous?

Elizabeth: I'm not jealous! I just—

Elizabeth stops short as she realizes that she is *jealous.*

Elizabeth: So what if I am? Does that make me a terrible person?

Asher: No.

Elizabeth: Just once, I'd like for a guy to notice *me.* Not her, me!

Asher: I noticed you. You're the first nice person, after Jesus, that ever helped me. Samantha screamed, but you brought me home. You're nice.

Elizabeth smiles, leans over, and hugs Asher.

Elizabeth: Thanks, Asher. I needed to hear that. I just wish someone else would see what you see.

Asher: No, never! I've seen bad things, scary things.

Elizabeth looks at Asher, not really knowing how to take him. She laughs, shakes her head, and stands back up.

Elizabeth: Well, I need to go open up shop. People will be showing up and will be wanting to do business. You can come out there if you want, or you can stick around here—it doesn't matter.

Asher: Outside for me!

A sudden thought strikes Elizabeth.

Elizabeth:	Asher, maybe you should stay inside . . . for today.
Asher:	Why?
Elizabeth:	Well, um, you might scare some of the customers.
Asher:	*(Softly.)* Oh.
Elizabeth:	I mean, you . . . it's just . . . I'll take you out for a walk later, OK? Just not right now.

Asher nods and crawls underneath the table and curls up in a ball.

Elizabeth:	I'm sorry, Asher.

Asher says nothing. Elizabeth exits.

Asher:	God, why am I so ugly? I thought You made only beauty. But people . . . I'm ugly. No one likes me. They're still scared of me.

Scene 4

Asher is still sitting under the table some four hours later when Darren enters, singing.

Darren:	"And I am why the Lord created men!"

Darren stops short when he spies Asher under the table.

Darren:	What have we here? What little vermin has crawled under our table?

*Darren throws the table over and Asher scrambles
away. Darren throws his head back and laughs.*

Darren:	Asher! What are you doing in here all by yourself? Stealing food?
Asher:	No! I have to stay inside or I'll scare the customers.
Darren:	Yes, you would do that, wouldn't you?
Asher:	I don't want to scare people.
Darren:	*(Patronizing tone.)* Asher, Asher, Asher. We all do things that we don't

want to do, but we have to do.

Asher: I *have* to scare people?

Darren: You can't help it; you're a freak. You crawl around like some deranged dog and talk like a child. You . . . you can't help but scare people.

Asher: Elizabeth's gonna help me not be freak!

Darren: And how do you think she's going to do that? Elizabeth doesn't have time for you. She has a business to run, with her father running off to Jerusalem for the Passover. He's always been a bit flighty.

Asher: But . . . but . . . why'd they bring me home if they don't have time for me?

Darren: Oh, 1,001 reasons. Maybe she'll sell you to some merchants, like Joseph's brothers did.

Asher: Sell me?

Darren: You're worth a few shekels! You're not the sharpest arrow in the quiver, but you'd make a good slave.

Asher: I'm no slave! Been there, done that, lived in a crypt.

Darren laughs.

Darren: Right, right. I heard about that little incident. You ran back home, and told everyone your story.

Asher: But no one ever listened.

Darren: No one listened to you? Have you no idea what you did to those people? Within a short time, everyone in Decapolis knew of your little exploit with that Jesus character and over 10,000 people turned from their religion to follow Him! It was mass hysteria! It was awful! Terrible! You single-handedly turned a good, God-fearing city of Jews into a place of degradation! Those people are nothing but Gentiles now!

Asher sits in total shock. He begins to smile. His smile grows larger until he is beaming.

Asher: I'm not a messer-upper! I helped Jesus!

Darren: Jesus? You want to help Jesus? You . . . you . . .

Asher turns and looks at Darren. The two of them study each other
for a long moment. Both are disgusted by what they see inside the other.

Asher: You're ugly.

Darren: (*Taken aback.*) Well you're not exactly a Ralph Lauren model yourself.

Asher: You have a bad heart. You're supposed to be good. You're supposed to be a leader. But instead, you let bad men make your heart bad.

Darren: I must be strong and not bend or break to this rebel, Jesus! If I, a very pillar of the community, were to fall into the hands of this madman, what would that say? How would *that* look?

Asher: At least the people would know the truth. You act like a friend; you smile a lot. But your heart is bad.

Darren: You listen to me, you twisted little twit. I don't care what you think you did. I don't care what you think you know about Samantha or Elizabeth. If they don't sell you off to Egypt, I will. You're nothing but a pest. We'd be *lucky* to make money off you, but I'd be willing to *pay them* to take you.

Asher: No . . .

Darren: Oh, yes!

Asher: (*Shouts.*) No!

Asher runs off stage, spilling the table's contents in the process. He is never
seen or heard from again. Darren smiles triumphantly and walks off stage.

<u>Scene 5</u>

Elizabeth and Samantha enter. They discover the mess spilled across the floor.

Samantha: What a mess! What happened in here?

Elizabeth: I don't know, but we'd better clean it up.

The girls talk throughout the rest of the scene as they clean up the stage.

If and when they finish cleaning up, they can sit at the table and continue talking.

Samantha: Do you think Asher did this?

Elizabeth: I can't imagine that he would. But he was the only one here.

Samantha: What did Darren want to talk to you about?

Elizabeth: Huh?

Samantha: Darren. He wanted to talk to you.

Elizabeth: I never saw him.

Samantha: Really? I ran into him at the market and he was asking about you. I said that you'd be out running the shop.

Elizabeth: He never came by.

Samantha: Oh, well.

A silent moment passes, then Samantha continues.

Samanatha: Elizabeth?

Elizabeth: Yeah?

Samantha: What are we gonna do with Asher? I mean, do you really foresee him staying here forever?

Elizabeth: I don't know. I've been thinking about it . . .

Samantha: And?

Elizabeth: I just don't know.

Samantha: Would it be so terrible if he did stay here with us?

Elizabeth: C'mon, Sam, think practically. How could we afford to put him up? We barely make enough as it is.

Samantha: I know but, well, what about *him?* Where is he gonna go? Who is he gonna turn to?

Elizabeth: I don't know.

Samantha: He has no friends, no family. We let him go and he's going to wander the streets as a homeless beggar. Or we could just take him back to the cemetery so he can scare the children at night and gnaw on rats when he gets hungry.

Elizabeth: Samantha—

Samantha: *(Interrupts.)* What are we going to do?

Elizabeth: *(Screams.)* I don't know!

Elizabeth's sudden outburst startles Samantha, and even Elizabeth can't believe that she just screamed the way she did. A silent moment passes. Samantha clears her throat.

Samantha: Sorry. I just . . . I just want to do something for him, you know? I want to help him. Give him a life again. Teach him how to walk and how to speak more maturely. Maybe help him get a job, so he could work his way back into society.

Elizabeth smiles, reaches over and squeezes Samantha's hand.

Elizabeth: I'll talk to Father when he gets home. We'll see, eh?

Scene 6

Father stumbles onto the stage, worn out from his long journey. He sets down his bags and stretches. Plopping down in one of the chairs at the table, he sighs contently. Elizabeth comes out, wrapped in a robe and yawning.

Elizabeth: Father?

Father: Elizabeth!

Father stands and the two hug.

Father: I'm sorry, did I wake you?

Elizabeth: I was just getting to bed when I heard your donkey knock over our water jugs *again*. They shattered didn't they? We'll have to buy new ones early tomorrow.

Father: Sorry I'm so late. The traffic coming out of Jerusalem was unbelievable. I've never seen it so busy. It was unbelievable—did I already say that? Well, it was unbelievable.

Elizabeth laughs.

Elizabeth: So how was the rest of the weekend?

Father: Different—very different. Everyone was talking about the death of Jesus.

Elizabeth: He died?

Father: Just this Friday. He was crucified by the Romans. Can you believe it? Everyone in Jerusalem couldn't. Some talked about how He was supposed to be the king of Israel, others talked about the miracles He performed. Some claimed that His kingdom is not an earthly one. Either way, no one could believe that He'd been dead.

Elizabeth: "Had been" dead?

Father: Yes, "had been" dead. He rose from the grave yesterday morning!

Elizabeth: *(Astonished.)* What?

Father: It's true! Everyone's talking about it. The priests are getting real scared and are telling people that His followers stole His body.

Elizabeth: How can a man rise from the dead? Father, I think you've been out in the sun a little too long. C'mon, let's get some sleep and—

Father: *(Interrupting.)* Elizabeth! You know as well as I do that this Jesus was no ordinary man. Don't you remember how He fed us with that basket of fish and bread? There were *thousands* of us there! And you heard all the same stories I did, about all the other miracles. This man truly was the son of God!

Samantha enters.

Samantha: Father! Welcome home.

Samantha hugs Father.

Samantha: Elizabeth, have you seen Asher?

Elizabeth: Isn't he in the spare room?

Samantha: No. I haven't seen him since this morning.

Darren marches on stage.

Father: Darren!

The girls try to cover themselves, as they are in robes and were just asleep moments ago.

Elizabeth: What are you doing, just barging in at this hour?

Darren: You really should invest in some locks. Of course, you don't even have any doors. Anyone can just walk in here . . . or out of here. Never mind. So, when are you going to start thanking me?

Father: Thanking you for what?

Darren: For driving that little pest out of the house. What was his name? Asher? Yeah, I chased him out of here. You won't be seeing him around here any longer.

A silent moment.

Elizabeth: *(Angry.)* Who gave you the right—

Samantha: *(Shocked and angry.)* You *what?*

Father: *(To Darren.)* Why?

Darren: Oh, please. Don't get all misty-eyed on me. You act like he needed you. He doesn't need you. He was using you. He's a wild animal; he can't live within these four walls. He—

Elizabeth: *(Interrupting.)* He's right.

Samantha: *(Astonished.)* What are you saying, sister?

Elizabeth: Asher didn't need us. We needed him.

Darren: Like a hole in the head.

Samantha: *(Screaming.)* Shut up, you good-for-nothing arrogant fool! You have everything—a home, a family, luxury. And what do you do for God? Nothing! But Asher? He has nothing! And what stops him from preaching the Gospel? Nothing! He has every excuse to just lock himself away from society, yet he tries; he really tries! What's your excuse?

Darren is stunned into silence. Finally, Elizabeth speaks.

Elizabeth: I'm going to get dressed.

Samantha: Me too.

Father: And where do you two think you're going at this hour?

Elizabeth: The cemetery, of course.

Darren: *(Rolls his eyes, nods, and speaks sarcastically.)* Of course.

The girls rush off stage. Father's countenance reflects deep thoughtfulness, then he speaks.

Father: *(Nodding; determined.)* Of course. *(Turns in the direction where the girls just exited and calls after them.)* Bring the large lamp. We'll need it.

24

DEATH ROW

THEME
Jesus
as Our
Substitute

PROPS AND NECESSITIES

✰ **Modern-day attire as described in play**
✰ **Chair**
✰ **Clipboard with several loose papers on it**
✰ **Hammer**
✰ **Spotlight**

SOUNDTRACKS
(if desired)

✰ *The Mummy*
✰ *Michael Collins*
✰ *Sleepy Hollow*

CAST

✰ **Gabriel**   ✰ **Rufus**
✰ **Nathia**   ✰ **Satius**
✰ **Barabbas**   ✰ **Miriam**
✰ **Hadassah**

Scene 1

Play music "The Mummy," track 1; fade out at 0:35. Lights on. The setting is a dark, dank jail cell. Barabbas is waiting impatiently at center stage, his arms crossed over his chest. Gabriel sits quietly at stage left, praying. As music fades out, Rufus and Nathia enter from stage right, dragging Satius with them. Satius is dressed very nicely and is very self-conscious about the way he looks. Satius struggles but to no avail. Barabbas laughs when the guards throw Satius to the floor.

Satius: You can't do this to me!

Barabbas: Actually, they can.

Nathia: *(To Barabbas.)* Jewish pig.

Barabbas: *(Snarls.)* Roman swine.

Nathia: You watch yourself Barabbas, or we'll—

Barabbas: Or you'll *what?* I'm already on death row!

Rufus: You're only making it worse for yourself.

Barabbas: Making it worse? How could I be making it worse? I'm going to be crucified!

Nathia and Rufus shake their heads, throw their hands in the air, and leave. Satius stands, brushing the dirt off his suit.

Satius: Ruffians.

Barabbas: Welcome to the end of your life.

Satius: Well don't set an extra place setting at dinner. I won't be here long.

Barabbas: Oh? You have plans tonight? A date with an Egyptian princess, perhaps?

Satius: I won't be here long.

Barabbas: Yeah, I heard you the first time. But I have a little tidbit of information for you. This ain't your local motel. This is death row. You're here for a reason, and the next time you walk through those doors, it'll be to pick up your cross or head to the gallows.

Satius: My friends won't let me die here.

Barabbas: Oh? You have friends in high places?

Satius: Let's just say they have this so-called government wrapped around the proverbial little finger.

Barabbas studies Satius for a moment.

Barabbas: Do I know you? You're lookin' real familiar to me right now.

Satius: I hardly think so.

Barabbas: Yeah, you're one of them priests, aren't ya'? I seen you at the temple. I think I even fell asleep during one of your sermons. Why are *you* here?

Satius: That, my friend, is none of your business.

Gabriel: The wages of sin is death.

Satius:	What?
Gabriel:	You act so surprised that you wound up here. Yet you've known for some time that the lifestyle you've been leading was going to sooner or later lead you right here.
Satius:	I have done nothing that deserves the death penalty!
Gabriel:	Breaking the Law, no matter how "small," is still breaking the Law.
Satius:	Don't you preach to me!
Barabbas:	That's right! *He's* the preacher! He doesn't get preached to; *he* does the preaching!
Gabriel:	But all have fallen short of the glory of God.
Barabbas:	Yeah, yeah, whatever. *(Turns to Satius.)* So what are you in for?
Satius:	I still cannot see how that's any of your business!
Gabriel:	There is coming a day when all of history will know your sins, and you're afraid to reveal them to this single convict?

Barabbas turns to Gabriel.

Barabbas:	Who *are* you?
Gabriel:	A lonely stranger. But this fellow, he's a gem. For years, he's stood behind the pulpit and preached the Word. For years, he's condemned every sin except his own greed. He dipped into the tithe collected, he hiked up prices on the sacrificial animals, he—
Satius:	*(Interrupting.)* That's not true!
Gabriel:	You mean to tell us that you're *not* here because of that audit?

Satius is stunned silent.

Barabbas:	Wow. I've done a lot of disgusting things in my time, but nothing like that man. That takes a lot of gall. Wow. And you're supposed to be a pillar of the community! I hope you spent the money well, 'cuz in the next

week or so, you're gonna hang!

Satius tries to ignore Barabbas.

Satius: How do you know all this?

Gabriel: I was there the whole time. I saw everything.

Satius: I don't remember . . .

Barabbas: Ya'll know who *I* am?

Satius: No.

Barabbas: You ain't never heard of Barabbas the Barbarian?

Satius: You're . . . *him?*

Barabbas: Oh yeah. Killed over 40 Roman soldiers, not counting women and children.

Gabriel: And you say that as if it's something to be proud of.

Barabbas: Listen, pal. I don't know who you are, but you're on my last nerve. If you don't shut up, I'm gonna come over there and slap your holier-than-thou mouth shut!

Gabriel doesn't say anything. He stares at Barabbas for a moment, as if sizing him up. With a shake of the head, he retreats to stage left and sits back down.

Satius: How can I be in the same cell as someone like you?

Barabbas: Weird, huh?

Satius: I'm a good person! Sure, I've made a few mistakes along the way, but nothing like you! I've never killed anybody! I've never stolen from anybody. Okay, so I hiked up the prices a bit, but who doesn't? And I'm clergy, so that tithe belongs to me anyway, right? What's the big deal?

Barabbas: Oh, you're right. You're as clean and innocent as a baby lamb.

Satius doesn't pick up on Barabbas' sarcasm.

Satius: Thank-you.

Barabbas turns to Gabriel.

Barabbas: Thick as a brick.

Scene 2

Rufus and Nathia enter, dragging a chair behind them. Rufus has a clipboard with several loose papers attached to it. Barabbas and Satius back away. Nathia crosses over and grabs Satius.

Rufus: We've got a few questions for ya' Satius.

Nathia sits Satius down in the chair.

Satius: I've got nothing to tell you. I already told them everything.

Rufus: We don't care about your sticky fingers.

Nathia: You were accused, tried, and convicted by your peers. That's why you're here. We're just providing a service.

Rufus: And quite frankly, we couldn't care less about your little Jewish problems. We have a much bigger, broader picture to worry about.

Satius: I don't know who you think you are, but—

Satius is cut off as Nathia grabs his throat.

Nathia: You Jews are all the same. Whining, complaining, and crying about our occupation in your country, not knowing how well you really have it. Did you know that you're the only country that we've ever allowed to keep their own religion? We let you perform your little services. Though you worship a god that doesn't answer your cries, though you follow blindly, we allow you to continue to do so because we don't want to have to put up with you if we were to take your privileges away. So I'd be thankful. You don't deserve it this well. You don't deserve your religion, you don't deserve this plush cell. You're a criminal, and you have no rights.

Rufus: So I wouldn't back talk her anymore.

Barabbas: Ooh, my kind of woman!

Satius is obviously shaken up. Nathia releases Satius and glares at Barabbas.

Satius: Wh-what questions do you have for me?

Rufus: That's better. For some time now, we've been monitoring the actions of a particular Nazarene named Jesus. He's been causing us some problems, stirring up mobs and a lot of anti-Roman feelings amongst your fellow countrymen.

Satius: Jesus?

Rufus: It's our understanding that you've had some contact with the man.

Satius: *(Pauses.)* So what if I have?

Rufus: Tell us about him.

Satius: I don't know how much I can really tell you, but I know the man's trouble. He came in one day not too long ago and started a riot in the synagogue.

Nathia: A riot?

Satius: I was there, just minding my own business, selling animals and what not, and he comes in and starts turning over tables. I've never seen someone so angry in all my life.

Rufus: What was he so angry about?

Satius: I dunno. It's not like we were doing anything out of the ordinary. He just showed up, started grabbing tables, throwing them this way and that, grabbing merchants, cracking his whip. Man, it was like something out of a movie.

Rufus: Do you think he was trying to prove a point?

Satius: Whad'ya mean?

Rufus: If you were going to start a riot to, say, overthrow the government, there are more strategic places to strike. Why the church? Did he say anything?

Satius: Something like "How dare you make my Father's house a den of thieves" or something like that. I don't know, I wasn't really listening.

Nathia:	And his followers? They joined in on the fighting?
Satius:	No, actually they didn't. They were just as stunned as everyone else. They just stood there on the sidelines and watched. They looked pretty horrorfied. Kinda funny, really.
Rufus:	So it was just Jesus against . . . everyone selling goods in the church hall? Was anyone killed? injured?
Satius:	No, nobody got hurt, not as far as I know.

Rufus turns away, facing the audience. He thumbs through the reports on his clipboard.

Rufus:	It just doesn't make any sense . . .
Nathia:	What?
Rufus:	Oh, nothing. Never mind. Come on, let's go.
Nathia:	You be a good Jewish boy now, and maybe we'll kill you quickly.

Rufus exits stage right, with Nathia dragging the chair off.

Barabbas:	They're so thoughtful and considerate, that's what I love most about them.
Satius:	What was all that about?
Gabriel:	They were obviously curious about Jesus, He who John described as "the Lamb of God, who takes away the sins of the world."
Barabbas:	Won't you just shut up?

Lights off. Play "Michael Collins" track 11. Fade out at 0:25.

Scene 3

As the music fades out, the lights come back on. All the prisoners are asleep except Gabriel, who's praying silently. There's a slight commotion off stage right, and Hadassah is suddenly flung onto the stage. This wakes the others up.

Satius:	A girl? In the same cell as us?

Barabbas: That's no girl—that's Hadassah.

Hadassah: Nice to see you too, Barabbas.

Barabbas: What brings a soft desert bloom such as yourself to a cold, cruel prison such as this?

Hadassah: They're cleaning out my cell, and all the other places are full, so here I am. Lucky me.

Baarabbas: So whatever happened to you? The guys really missed you.

Satius: (*Shocked.*) You were part of his gang?

Barabbas: She was more like . . . the in-flight entertainment.

Hadassah: That's a very nice way of putting it.

Satius: Oh, you're a whore.

Barabbas, enraged, grabs Satius. Gabriel leaps to his feet.

Barabbas: I don't care if it is the truth! You call her that again and they'll have to *kill* me to get me off of you! I don't care what her profession is or was. She's a lady, and she deserves your respect. Is that understood?

Satius: Yeah, perfectly.

Gabriel: Lessons in morality from a murderer.

This, too, enrages Barabbas. He spins around and begins moving toward Gabriel.

Barabbas: That's it, preacher man.

Gabriel holds up a solitary finger.

Gabriel: Don't.

He says it with such authority and power that it actually startles Barabbas, who stops and stands still. Staring at Gabriel for a moment, he turns back around when he hears Nathia enter from stage right. She marches straight to Hadassah.

Nathia: Are you causing trouble in here?

Hadassah: No.

Nathia: Don't lie to me, you wretch! No sooner have we brought you in here, and everyone's up in arms. The entire cellblock is complaining about all the racket!

Hadassah: It's just those guys! They're arguing and fighting—

Nathia: *(Interrupts.)* Over you, no doubt.

Hadassah: It's not my fault! It was you and your idiot captain that moved me in here. If you used the sense God gave a mule, you'd know—

Nathia: Ugly words from an ugly woman.

Hadassah: Now listen here . . .

Nathia: No, *you* listen. If we hear so much as another peep out of this cell, I will personally see to it that you are flayed, drawn, quartered, and left to rot in the streets. You have disgraced yourself, your family, and your community for far too long. I will not hesitate to see you publicly humiliated.

Gabriel: It wasn't her fault!

Nathia doesn't even notice Gabriel. Rufus enters.

Rufus: What's going on in here?

Nathia: Just putting a little fear into the neighborhood scum.

Rufus knows that Nathia has been, no doubt, acting in an uncalled for manner. He looks from Nathia to Hadassah and sighs.

Rufus: *(To Nathia.)* Go about your business.

Nathia: But—

Rufus: *(Interrupts.)* Go about your business!

Nathia stares at Rufus for a long moment, her arms crossed over her chest.

Muttering to herself, she marches off stage right.

Gabriel: It truly was not the girl's fault.

Rufus: You'll have to excuse Nathia. She's a little high-strung.

Hadassah: Oh, I know. She's always been like that, ever since we were little. Mom and Dad would be out of town on business or something, and Nathia would get in one of her moods and . . .

Hadassah struggles to continue.

Gabriel: Let it out.

Hadassah: *(With growing passion.)* I never wanted to be a prostitute! I never wanted my life to end like this. I just wanted to make them proud, that's all! I just wanted to make them proud, that's all! Mom and Dad were always so proud of Nathia. She was the straight A student, she was the one going off and joining the police force. But I was never able to measure up. I never was able to be the girl they wanted me to be. I never had the right friends, never wore the right clothes, never listened to the right music . . . I never saw it coming. One day, I'm off having fun with friends, and then suddenly four years have gone by. Mom's a widow, my sister's in charge of a Jewish garrison, . . . and I'm getting paid by strangers to destroy my dignity.

Rufus: I . . . um, well . . .

Hadassah: I knew it was wrong. I went to the priests, to see if they could help but—

Satius: *(Interrupts.)* See? That's the problem with this world. You get caught in a sticky situation, and you come running to the clergy, thinking we can fix everything. Well, we can't.

Gabriel: No, but there's a God Who can, and as a priest you should be directing those who seek help to Him.

For whatever reason, Rufus doesn't notice Gabriel nor pays any attention to what he says.

Barabbas: Whine, whine, whine. That's all you priests do.

Hadassah: Then one of my friends, Mary, came up to me and told me about this man she had met. His name was Jesus.

Rufus: Jesus?

Hadassah: Yeah. Mary came in one morning after a long night's work and told me about this guy and everything he'd done for her and how she's quitting the business and . . . I had to meet him. Anyone who could make Mary want to do a complete turn around like that . . . had to be something else.

Rufus: Well?

Hadassah: I never met him. I went out looking for him one night, and instead of finding him, I stumbled into some police officers who recognized me and they arrested me.

Rufus: Whatever happened to this Mary girl you mentioned?

Hadassah: She gave up the trade completely. Started following this Jesus around, from what I understand. I ran into her the morning before the night I was arrested, and she was just beaming. I had never seen her so happy. She didn't have on half the make-up she usually did, she wasn't wearing the same clothes, and she sure wasn't using the words she used to use. She was so different, so changed. But it was all for the good. *All for the good.* That's when I said "I have to meet this guy."

Rufus: Who is this Jesus? A revolutionary with a soft spot for low-lifes?

Hadassah: (*Sarcastically.*) You're too kind. The guy had to be more than a revolutionary. Our line of work isn't totally bad. We meet lots of men in our line of work; lots of men with charm, charisma, passion, you name it. But we don't let ourselves get involved. Somehow—without even doing business with Him—this guy totally rocked her world.

Rufus thinks about this for a moment longer and then quickly exits stage right.

Barabbas: What was that all about?

Satius: I wouldn't worry about it. They're gonna get that Jesus. I know my friends well. They'll have him dangling from a noose before his next birthday.

Barabbas: Who asked anything about that?

Gabriel: But he speaks the truth. It is for you, all of you, that this Jesus you speak of will die. He has come to fulfill the prophecies of old. But you refuse to see Him. You, Satius the priest, are too consumed with greed and laziness to ever care enough for the world around you. That is why He must die. Hadassah, your suspicions were right. Jesus is no normal man. But unless you leave your life of sin, you will never see Jesus in glory. And you, Barabbas, will have the heaviest cross to carry, although you will not carry one at all. Instead, you will face every day of the rest of your life knowing that Jesus took your place. You are all here on death row because of the lives you've led. But you do not have to face the eternal consequences if you don't want to. That is why God is love . . . and God is grace.

Barabbas: Who are you?

Gabriel: They call me Gabriel.

Gabriel walks off stage right with everyone staring in silence. Suddenly, Satius has some inkling of what just happened. He rushes to stage right.

Satius: Centurion! Centurion!

Rufus enters.

Rufus: What is it?

Satius: A man just escaped! He walked right out of the cell . . . right through the door!

Rufus looks around.

Rufus: Yet, somehow, you're all still here.

Lights out.

Scene 4

Play "Sleepy Hollow" track 1; fade out at 0:40. As music fades out, a mob can be heard (either previously recorded or acted out off stage). There's lots of angry shouting, until slowly the chanting takes control of the whole crowd.

Mob: Crucify Him! Crucify Him!

The prisoners all wake up and look around, alarmed and frightened, not knowing what's going on.

Mob: Give us Barabbas! Give us Barabbas!

Barabbas: Lynch mob! I never saw this one coming! I know we don't live forever, but I never thought I'd be taken out by some of my own! Can you believe it? After everything I've done for them! All the blood spilled by me and my boys for their freedom! They want to kill me!

Rufus and Nathia enter and throw Miriam to the floor.

Rufus: C'mon Barabbas, you're coming with us.

Barabbas: You're gonna just turn me over to them?

Satius: Even as much as I dislike him, isn't there a law against this?

Rufus: You've been pardoned.

Hadassah: *(Stunned.)* What?

Nathia: Someone's taking your place.

Barabbas: What? I-I don't understand.

Rufus: Jesus of Nazareth is going to be carrying the cross carved for you.

Miriam: No!

Barabbas: *(Comes to some sudden realization.)* No, no, no! That's *my* cross!

Satius: The man is giving you a "Get out of Jail Free" card. You don't turn it down.

Hadassah: But Jesus instead of Barabbas? What kind of deal is that?

Miriam: Jesus doesn't deserve this and you know it! He's innocent!

Rufus: This is out of my hands.

Nathia: If we had it our way, we'd string up all of you.

Nathia grabs Barabbas.

Rufus: Take him out of here and give him to the crowd.

Barabbas, in a state of shock, is led off stage. Rufus approaches Miriam.

Rufus: What do you mean, he's innocent?

Hadassah: What is *she* in here for?

Satius: Do we really want to know?

Miriam: Disturbing the peace.

Rufus: She was leading a mob in protest to the crucifixion of the Nazarene. Why do you say he's innocent?

Miriam: You don't know Him like I do. He's not a revolutionary—He's the Messiah!

Satius: Don't be absurd. Don't you think that we, the priests, would have spotted the Messiah?

Rufus: While you were busy stealing tithe envelopes? Not likely.

Miriam: You think He's the Messiah too?

Rufus: No! I mean, how could . . . there's no such thing as . . . But how could something like this happen? And here, of all places?

Miriam: Centurion, my son, Reuben, was dead. Died in a cart accident. My husband died many years ago, fighting the Romans—no offense. Jesus came by our funeral procession, saw my son lying there dead, and commanded him to come back to life! My son was dead, but now he's alive because of Jesus! Jesus didn't come to usurp the throne! He came to bring life!

Rufus is tangled with mixed emotions and feelings. He rushes off the stage.
All the lights go off and the stage clears. Rufus reenters,
a spotlight hits him as he's holding a hammer and looking upward.

Rufus: Surely this *was* the Son of God.

25

FRIENDS FOREVER

THEME
Dating and
Friendship

PROPS AND NECESSITIES

☆ 3 Tables
☆ 6 Chairs
☆ Server's apron
☆ Serving tray
☆ Lots of loose papers
☆ Pen
☆ 2 glasses

 CAST

☆ Josh
☆ Sarah
☆ Luke
☆ Doug
☆ Tiffany
☆ Alex

Scene 1

The setting is a college campus snack shop. The stage is set with a table at back center stage, a table at stage left and a table at stage right. Two chairs are at each table. Josh enters wearing a server's apron. He begins cleaning the tables. Sarah enters from stage left and sits down at the table on stage right. She impatiently pounds on the table.

Sarah: Could I *puh-leeze* have a server over here?

Josh sighs, waxes on a smile, turns around, and approaches Sarah's table.

Josh: Welcome to Feed Yer Face. What can I get for you this afternoon?

Sarah: You, and every other man on the face of this planet, can just go off to some far away island and die! And take all your pit bulls and Doberman pinchers with you!

Josh: I'm sorry, that's not on the menu. Maybe

you'd like the soup of the day?

Sarah: Oh . . . that is so like you men. Always a witty comeback, always think you're so smart, don't ya'? I hate men. I *loathe* men. Are you a man?

Josh: (*Under his breath.*) Never in all my life have I been so tempted to tell an untruth.

Sarah: Sit down!

  Josh, scared and intimidated, quickly sits in the other chair.

Josh: Yes ma'am.

Sarah: What is it with men and commitment? I mean, is it such a terrible thing? Why is it that when we just mention the word, you go running and screaming into the hills?

Josh: You can't generalize all men like that!

Sarah: Why not?

Josh: Because not all men are like that.

Sarah: Oh yeah? Name one who isn't.

Josh: I know this one guy who was head-over-heels in love with this girl. They had been dating for, like, six months and he decides to pop the question. Except, when he goes to find her, he finds his love in the arms of another man.

Sarah: Well, I'm sure he drove her to it.

Josh: No, this was totally unprovoked. He would have done anything for her. She was just a bad girl.

Sarah: Really?

Josh: Really.

Sarah: Wow. Sounds like I might need to meet this friend of yours.

Josh:	Oh, well, you can't.
Sarah:	Why not?
Josh:	He doesn't exactly live around here.
Sarah:	So give me his e-mail address.
Josh:	I can't.
Sarah:	Why not? He *does* exist, doesn't he?
Josh:	Of course he does! It's just that—
Sarah:	*(Interrupting.)* What?
Josh:	Alright, alright! I saw it on TV.
Sarah:	Uh-huh.
Josh:	I didn't want to see the movie. My ex-girlfriend made me sit through this stupid romantic made-for-TV movie about this guy who falls for this no-good woman who ditches the guy and runs off with an airline pilot who flys her to Nome, Alaska, where the no good girl leaves the pilot for a blubbery Eskimo.
Sarah:	I dunno, but the storyline sounds totally unrealistic.
Josh:	That's why girls like 'em.
Sarah:	What?
Josh:	Is that my boss calling?

Josh jumps up and exits stage right. Luke and Doug enter stage left.

Luke:	Don't get me started man, I'm telling you, women find me both exciting *and* fascinating.
Doug:	Whatever.

Luke and Doug sit at the table at stage left. Luke sits in the chair facing center stage while Doug has his back to center stage.

Luke: They do!

Doug: So, Mister History Buff—and I use that last word loosely—when you tell them about how Utah was the thirty-seventh state to join the Union, which do they find that: exciting or fascinating?

Luke stares for a silent moment.

Luke: I only discussed Utah once.

Doug: Hey, you should at least save Utah for the second date. You don't want to be too exciting the first time around. What'll you do for the *second* act?

Luke notices Sarah.

Doug: Whoa, who's that?

Doug turns around and sees Sarah as well.

Doug: Hey, she's a pretty mama!

Luke: As in totally!

Doug: She's mine.

Doug stands but Luke pulls him back down.

Luke: Dude, I saw her first!

Doug: But I *acted* first!

Luke: Only because I pointed her out!

Doug: You snooze, you lose. She's mine.

Luke: OK, OK. Here's the deal.

Doug: What? No! There is no "deal." She's mine!

Luke: You wanna settle this like hormonally charged boys or like men?

Doug:	Which am I?
Luke:	Please don't make me answer that.
Doug:	Alright, what's the deal?
Luke:	We'll call Josh over here. When he comes to the table, if he says, "Yeah, whatcha want?" she's yours. But if he comes and says, "Whazzup?" she's mine.
Doug:	Ok, that's fair.

Doug and Luke bang on the table.

Doug/Luke:	Server! We need a server!

Josh enters from stage right, obviously annoyed.

Josh:	Well, if is isn't the Desperate Duo. What do you want?

Doug and Luke stare at each other, and then look up to Josh.

Luke:	That's it?
Doug:	Aren't you gonna ask us what we want?
Luke:	Or whazzup?
Josh:	You called me over. I came over. You want something or not? I'm not really in the mood for funny stuff at the moment.
Doug:	C'mon, ask me what I want so I can go ask that gorgeous girl out!

Josh points to Sarah.

Josh:	Her?
Doug:	How many other gorgeous girls do you see in this pitiful excuse for a restaurant?
Josh:	I was just talking with her.

Luke: Dude, really? What is she like? Is she as nice as she looks?

Josh: I don't know. She bit my head off so quickly, I wasn't able to tell.

Doug: You know what, Luke? I've been thinking. You can have her.

Luke: I will, thank-you very much.

Doug looks up at Josh.

Doug: That's one stupid sibling you have there.

Josh: He's your brother too.

Doug: Yeah, but he's from your side of the family.

Tiffany enters from stage left, marching quickly off toward stage right.

Tiffany: *(To Josh.)* You're not standing around talking to customers, are you?

Josh: No, Miss Tiffany Boss Ma'am! I was just taking their order . . . sort of.

Josh exits stage right. Luke stands, takes in a deep breath,
and crosses the stage. Sarah doesn't notice him until he clears his throat.

Sarah: Yes, man-thing?

Luke: I couldn't help but notice you sitting over here by yourself and—

Sarah: *(Interrupting.)* And *what?* You thought you could just waltz on over here, order me a chocolate fudge sundae, and all my worries would be gone? Hey, maybe you could even get my telephone number! But why bother? It's not like you're going to call! Sure, maybe you will tonight, and when you drive me home you'll promise to call, but you won't. So let's just save ourselves the time. Order me a lemon water, I'll smile, I'll dump you, and then you can go back to your friend there and brag about how big and macho you are and how you couldn't let someone like me drag you down any longer!

Luke stands for a silent moment, turns around, and sits back down with Doug.

Luke: *(To Doug.)* She's yours.

Doug: You mentioned Utah, didn't you?

Luke: No.

Doug: Louisiana Purchase?

Luke: As a matter of fact, I did not.

Doug: I'm impressed! Now watch and see how a pro handles it. Feel free to take notes.

Doug stands up, stretches slightly, and begins strutting over to Sarah's table.

Sarah: *(To Doug.)* Just because you're cuter than your failure of a friend doesn't mean I owe you anything. Just buy me ice cream, candy, and chocolates, then compare my eyes to the moonlight. Don't all girls melt under those conditions? Use me and abuse me, that's all I'm good for! Listen to me, you stunted little slime, I wouldn't date you if you were the last man on earth!

Doug: How about some time after that?

Sarah stares at Doug.

Sarah: I'll think about it.

Doug: I bet you will. *(Hands paper to Sarah.)* Here's my cell number.

Sarah: Oh, which prison are you in?

Doug: It's my phone number.

Sarah: No, that's ok. I already have it.

Doug: Saw my picture in the student directory, huh?

Sarah: Yeah. I'll call you later, sometime after the nuclear holocaust.

Doug: I'm looking forward to it.

Doug, pasting on a confident smile, swaggers back and sits back down with Luke. Luke stares at Doug, not sure what to make of him. Finally Doug speaks to Luke.

Doug: See how simple that was? Historical facts never once entered the conversation. There was that little bit about a nuclear holocaust, but that's to be expected when you first meet. You'll be my best man, and I'll name our first son after you.

Luke: You are not my brother.

Doug: I've been sayin' the same thing for years.

Alex enters, piles of loose papers in her hands. She throws them down on the middle table and sighs in relief. She spots the guys.

Alex: Oh, Doug! Luke! Perfect! I could totally use your help right now.

Luke: Uh, sure Alex, what's up?

Alex: Ok, I have this children's church thing I have to put together, and I'm trying to decide which story to present.

Doug: What are the options?

Alex: Adam and Eve . . .

Luke: Too risky.

Alex: Gideon and the Midianites . . .

Doug: Too much violence.

Luke: I'm not sure how to put this, Alex . . .

Doug: Your ideas stink!

Luke: Mr. Sensitivity strikes again.

Alex: But they're some of my favorite stories!

Luke: And they teach us a lot, too. But the content might be a little . . . heavy for children.

Alex: So what do you suggest? A whimsical peek into the book of Revelation?

Doug: Go with something simple, like David, the dude who killed Goliath.

Luke: Or about how he was a shepherd boy.

Doug: Yeah. Your theme could be, "Little guys can do big things too!"

Alex: Hey, that's perfect! *(Picks up some of the papers, showing them to Doug and Luke.)* Thanks, guys!

Luke: No problem. Hey, Doug, it's time for us to get outta here.

Doug: Why?

Luke: We gotta go.

Doug: Where?

Luke: Does it matter? Let's go!

> *Doug and Luke exit stage left. Alex notices*
> *Sarah sitting beside herself. Alex strolls over.*

Alex: So who was the scum bag this time?

Sarah: Excuse me?

> *Alex sits down opposite Sarah.*

Alex: I know that look. It's the "I'm-So-Helpless-and-All-Alone-Because-My-Wannabe-Boyfriend-Just-Broke-My-Heart-Again-and-I-Hope-People-Pay-Attention-to-Me-and-Ask-Me-Questions-but-If-They-Do-I'll-Bite-Their-Head-Off-Because-They-Should-Know-Better" look.

Sarah: You could tell all that from way over there?

Alex: Oh, please. It was *so* obvious.

Sarah: You're good.

Alex: I know. By the way, my name's Alexandria Cordelia Fitzgerald, but everyone calls me Alex.

Sarah: I'm Sarah McCormick.

Alex: You don't sound Irish, but that's ok. I won't hold it against you, faker. So, what's the matter? What's the problem and what's his name?

Sarah: Brad.

Alex: Football player?

Sarah: Rugby.

Alex: So what did this wretched rugby-er do to you?

Sarah: It's not what he did. It's what he *didn't* do.

Alex: What didn't he do?

Sarah: It was our fourth anniversary today.

Alex: Wow! You've been dating for four years?

Sarah: Four weeks. And I got him this little stuffed rabbit, and it's holding this little red heart with lace all around it and on the heart it says "Some bunny loves you." And what did he give me? A stupid hug between quantum mechanics and sociology 101.

Alex: Wow, you've got serious problems.

Sarah: I'll say. What should I do?

Alex: First of all, turn off the sap tap—you're making me sick. Second, you need some balance in your life. This rugby player Brad has way too much influence on your life, especially for someone who's been seeing you for just four weeks. Look at me, for example. Do you see me flipping out over a bunch of little boy toys?

Sarah: I don't even know you.

Alex: See, wait, OK. Have you ever read the Bible?

Sarah: A little bit.

Alex: Ok. Do remember a little part that says "Seek ye first the kingdom of God, and all this shall be added unto you?"

Sarah: Vaguely.

Alex: Good. What He's saying is that if we strive for God and to fulfill His will, He'll take care of everything else. Even introducing us to Mister Right *(Turns toward audience.)* or Ms. Right, for you guys out there.

Sarah: So you're not dating anybody? You kissed dating goodbye?

Alex: I'm just not dating right now. I have other priorities right now. But I'm happy!

Sarah: Sure, that's easy for you to say. You don't *want* to date!

Alex: Sure I do! I love seeing those boys squirm behind their little tuxedos while they try to impress me! But like I said, the time isn't right for me.

Sarah: Are you serious? And this works for you?

Alex: Yep. Give God a try. You'll be surprised.

Sarah: So, what? Should I break up with him?

Alex: I can't answer that one! Pray about it. Didn't you hear a word I just said? God will help you know what to do.

Sarah: Well, could you maybe write down some verses for me or something? Things I can look up?

Alex grabs a piece of paper from the bottom of the stack on the other table and yanks it out. Papers fly everywhere. She retrieves a pen from behind her ear and begins writing. Sarah looks over Alex's shoulder. Tiffany Boss enters, with Josh close behind. She sees the papers and goes ballistic.

Tiffany: Josh, do you think we're running a dump here?

Josh: No, I—

Tiffany: *(Interrupting, pointing to the papers.)* Papers, *now!*

Tiffany approaches Sarah and Alex as Josh begins gathering the papers off the floor, straightening them back up on the table. Tiffany speaks again.

Tiffany: *(To Sarah.)* Can I get you anything?

Sarah: A cherry-vanilla soda.

Tiffany: *(To Alex.)* And for you?

Alex: Water on the rocks, straight up.

Tiffany exits stage right. Josh glances up from his papers and notices Alex. He stops and his jaw drops. He stares at her and drops the papers. Never taking his eyes off her, he slowly rises and sits down at the middle table. Tiffany comes back out with beverages on a tray. She serves Sarah and Alex. Josh begins working again. Tiffany approaches him.

Tiffany: What was *that* all about?

Josh: What was what?

Tiffany: I saw you staring.

Josh: I wasn't staring at Alexandria! Ok, maybe I was . . . a little.

Tiffany: You like her?

Josh: Like? No, I don't like her! *(Passionate and dreamy-eyed.)* I *love* her!

Tiffany: No way! You? Her? Well, I could see it, actually. Wow, this is so weird. She's my best friend!

Josh: Yeah, I know. That's why you have to swear that you heard nothing!

Tiffany: What? Why don't you just go over there and tell her?

Josh: What, and let her know that I like her? Are you insane?

Tiffany: C'mon, what's the worst that could happen?

Josh: I could die.

Tiffany: Oh, come on.

Josh: No . . . I . . . I don't think I could handle that kind of rejection.

A sense of realization suddenly comes over Josh.

Josh: But hey, you're her best friend! You could talk to her!

Tiffany: Uh, no.

Josh: Oh, come on! You don't have to ask her point-blank whether or not she would go out with me. Just casually bring my name up. Say something like, "Hey, that gorgeous hunk Josh is still single. Can you believe it? A good-looking guy like him? He's so charming and funny and caring and sensitive!" You know, something honest and disarming but not too flattering.

Meanwhile, on the other side of the stage . . .

Alex: OK, that's it!

Alex hands Sarah the paper.

Sarah: Wow, that looks like a lot.

Alex: Yeah, but they don't take long to read.

Sarah: Thanks a lot. Well, I'd better be going. See you later?

Alex: Sure, yeah, I'm around.

Sarah exits stage left. Alex stands up, looks around, and approaches Tiffany and Josh.

Tiffany: Hey, Alex.

Alex: Take a break, Tiff' dear. You look exhausted, not to mention totally stressed.

Tiffany: I am!

Alex: See? I knew that. I can see things like that.

Tiffany: What about Josh here? What do you see when you look at him?

Alex regards him for a moment. Josh is nervous and squeamish.

Alex: *(To Josh.)* Yeah, you'd be happy to pick up all my papers and take them to the dumpster out back for me, wouldn't you, love?

Josh: Oh yeah! Sure! No problem!

Alex: There's a good lad. Ta-ta!

Alex exits stage left.

Tiffany: You're never that cooperative with me.

Josh: Yeah, well, you're not her.

Tiffany: Clean all this up, mop up, then lock up. I'll see you tomorrow.

Tiffany exits stage left. Josh kicks the papers to the side and exits stage right.

Scene 2

Tiffany enters from left. Seeing the papers still scattered, she sighs.

Tiffany: If you want something done right, you gotta do it yourself!

As she begins to pick them up, Sarah enters.

Sarah: Hey, is Alex around?

Tiffany: Not yet, but she usually comes here around this time. You're welcome to wait.

Sarah: Yeah, that'd be good.

Sarah sits down at the far right table.

Tiffany: You're friends with Alex?

Sarah: She's been giving me advice. I've had some guy troubles.

Tiffany: Welcome to the club. But yeah, she's great with that stuff.

Sarah: Well, yeah, but . . . I don't think it's working.

Tiffany:	Oh yeah?

Josh enters.

Josh: Hello all you happy people!

Tiffany: *(To Sarah.)* One second. *(Turns to Josh.)* You are late! Now get to work! Pick up these papers! And how many times have I told you I want these tables arranged in 47-degree angles, off the middle table? And the middle table is to be exactly perpendicular to the wall, with the chairs sitting in an easterly position! C'mon, honestly, what am I paying you for? *(Turns back to Tiffany.)* So anyway, I'm Tiffany, and you are . . .

Josh begins picking up the papers. He continues to straighten up the snack shop as the girls talk..

Sarah: Sarah. And, well, Alex told me to pray about it, you know? And I did, but things haven't changed! I'm sitting here waiting for God to intervene, and He hasn't!

Tiffany: You can't just pray about it and then expect God to control your life with a remote control. He still expects you to think. That's partly how He talks to you.

Sarah: Really?

Tiffany: Sure. *(To Josh.)* You call that a 47-degree angle? Try again! *(To Sarah.)* You pray for these things and God *will* answer you, but you have to look for the answers. You have to read His Word, think about it and, you know, study it. Really soak it in. Think about how God handles various situations, and when you pray to Him, the answers will come to you. He'll reveal His will to you—through your life, your friends, the Bible, anything and everything. *(To Josh.)* Easterly! The chairs are supposed to be arranged easterly! That is so southwestern!

Josh: *(To Tiffany.)* I just want you to know, that the only reason I don't retaliate sarcastically or quit my job is because you are such a pretty woman and such a good friend.

Tiffany: That and I won't talk to Alex if you do.

Josh: Please! I'll never ask anything of you again!

Doug and Luke enter from stage left and sit at the left table. Josh quickly pulls up a chair and sits down with them. During the rest of this scene the girls and guys each keep to themselves. NOTE: When the guys talk, the girls freeze and vice-versa.

Doug: What's it take to get a soda around here?

Luke: And could we get some music? There's usually music here.

Josh: Soda fountain down and the CD player skips. I need some help, some advice.

Doug: And you're coming to *us*?

Luke: Dude must be desperate.

Guys freeze, cut to the girls.

Sarah: I suppose you're right, I just wish it was a little easier, you know? I don't need a burning bush; maybe just a fiery flower or a sparkling ivy. But something where I could say, "Oh, so *that's* the answer. Thanks!"

Tiffany: Sometimes it is that simple. Sometimes the truth just smacks you up-side the head, and you can't believe it never occurred to you before. But sometimes it's a little harder.

Cut to guys.

Josh: Ok, here's the thing . . .

Alex enters, and Josh pauses to watch her walk by.

Alex: Hello, my girls. How is everything in my favorite little college campus snack shop?

Sarah: Good.

Tiffany: Pretty great, actually. Just talking about guys and God.

Cut to guys.

Josh: Guys, just listen to me. I've got girl trouble.

Luke: Join the club.

Josh: Have you ever been so in love with a girl that it hurts?

Doug: Kimberly Cruise.

Josh: She impaled you with her ski pole!

Doug: I was in love and it hurt!

Luke: C'mon, Doug. Josh needs us right now. I can tell by the way his right eye is twitching.

Cut to girls.

Sarah: Tiffany was just explaining to me about how God answers prayers.

Alex: Oh, yeah. He works in mysterious ways, you know. One time, no joke, I received an answer through a leaf! A leaf! I was just looking at it and it was like, "Aha!"

Cut to guys.

Josh: Have you ever liked a girl—loved a girl—and wanted to tell her, but didn't know how to?

Luke: Yeah, that happened to me. Remember Katie Loskowitz? Well, I had a thing for her like you wouldn't believe. I mean, I was always thinking about her. I'd see the sun sparkling off that creek down by the boy's dorm, and it would remind me of her baby blue eyes. And at night, when the moon came out . . .

Josh: Focus, Luke, focus.

Luke: Well, anyway, I had written a couple of poems for her and, well, I decided that I should tell her. So I did. I marched up to her, handed her the poems and told her everything!

Josh: Wow. How'd it turn out?

Doug: Restraining order.

Cut to girls.

Alex: Guys can be such a hassle!

Tiffany: Sure, but you have to admit that life would be dull without them.

Alex: True.

Sarah: Yeah, what would we talk about?

Tiffany: Speaking of guys, Alex, have you ever noticed Josh?

Alex: Sure. He hangs out with us all the time.

Tiffany: Yeah. Well, last night as I'm walking home, I'm thinking, *How is it that he's remained unattached for so long? He's a great guy.*

Cut to guys.

Josh: Ok, so, well, you know Alexandria?

Luke: Sure. During the First Crusade—

Josh: Do you really think I care about the First Crusade? I'm talking about Alex!

Cut to girls.

Alex: Really?

Sarah: Who's Josh?

Tiffany: That guy over there, talking to his brothers. The one with the server's apron on.

Alex: You like him, Tiff?

Tiffany: No, well, I mean, not like that. You know I was just thinking that . . . you know. What do *you* think of him?

Alex: He's nice enough. But I'm not attracted to him in any way.

Cut to guys.

Josh: I think about her all the time!

Cut to girls.

Alex: He's charming, kinda funny.

Cut to guys.

Josh: She's the last thing I think about at night and the first thing I think about in the morning!

Cut to girls.

Alex: He's got a good heart.

Cut to guys.

Josh: She's so quirky and crazy. But she has that connection with God, ya' know?

Cut to girls.

Alex: He's the kind of guy you marry. I could marry him, but date him? Nah.

Cut to guys.

Josh: I'm not talking about a long-term commitment here. Just a date. See how it goes, ya' know? But yet, with her . . . I could see it going the distance.

Doug: *Marriage?*

Cut to girls.

Sarah: *Marry him?*

Cut to guys.

Luke: Whoa.

Cut to girls.

Tiffany: Oh.

Cut to guys.

Josh: So, should I do it?

Doug: Marry her before your first date? I don't know . . .

Cut to girls.

Alex: I don't know what I'd do if he asked me out, not that he would.

Cut to guys.

Josh: I'm gonna do it! What do I have to lose?

Luke: You could die.

Josh: I once thought as you do.

Luke: Dude, don't. Girls aren't worth it. You don't want to get tied down.

Sarah: Besides, it's not like we want to be tied down.

Sarah and Luke pause and turn toward each other.

Luke/Sarah: *(In unison.)* What?

Sarah: Were you listening to our conversation?

Luke: No. *(To other guys.)* Were you?

Josh: *(Stuttering.)* Why-why-why? What are you talking about over there?

Alex: Guys. What are you talking about?

Doug: Girls.

Tiffany: What were you saying?

Luke: *(Looking directly at Sarah.)* That they're not worth it. We don't need the hassle or stress.

Sarah: That's what we were saying about guys.

Luke: Oh, really . . .

Doug: Everyone knows girls are so much more of a headache than guys are!

Sarah: But guys are more insensitive!

Luke: Girls are *too* sensitive!

Alex: Guys have cooties!

Josh: Well, let's face it. There are these two extremes when it comes to women. We either love you or we hate you.

Doug: Women. Can't live with them, can't kill 'em.

Josh: And you women have the power to make us jump over this incredible abyss from love to hate at a moment's notice.

Alex: Yeah, well, if it *was* love, it wouldn't be so easily swayed.

Luke: She has a point.

Josh: I know that. And my feelings are unwavering.

Alex: What?

Tiffany: Uh, Josh, maybe—

Josh: (*Continuing.*) That's right, Alexandria.

Doug: Uh, dude . . .

Josh: I love you! And I'm not afraid to say it! I want the whole world to know that I am crazy about you!

Moment's silence.

Alex: Wow, Josh, I didn't see that one coming. But . . .

Luke: Oooh . . . the dreaded "B" word.

Alex: But I'm just not ready for any kind of relationship right now. I'd still like to be friends, though.

Moment's silence. Josh turns back toward his brothers.

Josh: I am going to die.

Tiffany: *(To Josh.)* Sorry . . .

Josh tries to remain strong, but fails miserably.

Josh: It's not like I needed the heartbreak, I mean, headache. No big deal. It's a big ocean and there are lots of fish in it. I'll heal, not that I'm wounded or anything.

Josh exits stage right. Alex turns to the girls.

Alex: Wasn't that the most pitiful thing you've ever seen? I mean, how could I be so cruel and callused and . . . But I'm just not ready. Not yet.

Sarah: Does anyone have his phone number? *(Everyone turns to Sarah.)* Just curious.

Alex: You think he's gonna be OK?

Luke: Josh? Yeah, he's always been the strongest of us all. He'll be fine. Nothing that a little prayer time, brotherly love, and a millennium or two can't fix.

Alex: Ooh, hey! But if you do see him, tell him that maybe I'll get back to him on that, OK? Maybe not right now, but maybe, when I'm like thirty and want to get married and have kids and everything, I'll give him a call.

Doug: If you want *good-looking* children, *I'm* the one to call.

Sarah: And you all just continue on? You're all still friends and everything?

Tiffany: Well, yeah.

Sarah: Won't it be kinda weird?

Alex: For a while, yeah.

Luke: But after those initial, awkward first 10 years are over with, everything will be back to normal.

Sarah:	Has *anything* ever torn you apart?
Doug:	The last piece of olive and pineapple pizza. No, not really. We have our arguments and everything, but nothing that lasts.
Luke:	That's the cool thing about being friends with God.
Doug:	Everything passes. You realize that you're a sinner who's gonna make mistakes and so are all of your friends. You can't stay upset with them.
Alex:	Not when Christ is the center point of your life. Hey I gotta go call Josh. We really ought to talk about all this. Oh, and hey, when I get back, you can tell me what you think about my new song!
Tiffany:	New song?
Alex:	Yeah, I wrote it for children's church. It's about David the shepherd boy. OK, actually it's more about his sheep. *(Alex exits, singing.)* Smelly sheep, smelly sheep, what are they feeding you? Smelly sheep, smelly sheep, it's not your fault!
Doug:	If she does ever end up as part of our family, I'm not going to admit it.

(All exit.)